The 1st Canadians
at War

The 1st Canadians at War

Two Accounts of the First Canadian Division in the Great War

From the St. Lawrence to the Yser With the 1st Canadian Brigade

by Frederic C. Curry

"Crumps" the Plain Story of a Canadian Who Went

by Louis Keene

LEONAUR

The 1st Canadians at War: Two Accounts of the
First Canadian Division in the Great War
From the St. Lawrence to the Yser With the 1st Canadian Brigade
by Frederic C. Curry
"Crumps": The Plain Story of a Canadian Who Went
by Louis Keene

Leonaur is an imprint of Oakpast Ltd

Material original to this edition and
presentation of text in this form
copyright © 2010 Oakpast Ltd

ISBN: 978-1-84677-982-4 (hardcover)
ISBN: 978-1-84677-981-7 (softcover)

http://www.leonaur.com

Publisher's Notes

Contents

FROM THE ST. LAWRENCE TO THE YSER WITH
THE 1ST CANADIAN BRIGADE

Preface   11
Ante-Bellum   13
Petewawa   18
Mobilisation   25
Val Cartier   29
The Convoy   33
In England   39
Interim   44
Ypres, 1915   47
With the Draft   53
The Breaking In   58
Reserve Billets   62
Bailleul   68
The Trek South   72
Festubert, 1915   77
Carpe Diem   81
Givenchy, 1915   85
Northward Again   94
Nights of Gladness!   99
In Front of Messines   105
Mine Warfare   109
Myths, Fairies, Etc.   113
The Winter Months   119
Epilogue   124

"CRUMPS" THE PLAIN STORY OF
A CANADIAN WHO WENT

Preface   127
"Crumps   129

From the St. Lawrence to the Yser With the 1st Canadian Brigade

Frederic C. Curry

Lieuts. Klotz, Strathy and Curry at Amesbury

To
Lieut.-General Sir Sam Hughes, K.C.B., M.P.
Minister of Militia
to whose efforts the efficiency of the Canadian
contingents is largely due.

Preface

In presenting this little work to the public the writer wishes to thank those of his fellow-officers and others who brought to his notice incidents that did not come under his personal observation.

Valuable assistance has been gained from the official accounts of Sir Max Aitken, and from the historical writings of Mr. John Buchan with regard to the parts played by other brigades and divisions with which we were co-operating.

In spite of these attempts to broaden its outlook, the book stands in the main a personal account of the actions of the 1st Brigade, Canadian Infantry.

As such, however, the writer hopes it will be accepted, and not as a detailed history of the events chronicled, though every attempt has been made to check the accuracy of the facts stated.

One fictitious character has been introduced, that of Begbie Lyte, in order to make the tale impersonal.

In all other cases the true names of persons mentioned, or initials, have been used.

To Dr. Shipley, Master of Christ's College, Cambridge, the writer owes much for his kindly criticisms and encouragement in this work.

F. C. Curry.
October, 1916.

CHAPTER 1

Ante-Bellum

Before the war the Canadian Militia consisted of about 75,000 of all ranks and all grades of efficiency. To a neutral eye it must have appeared to be in a highly disorganised condition, for battalions and corps had sprung up here and there throughout the country with no proportion existing between them and the other arms of the service. And yet within a short two months after the outbreak of hostilities a complete division, armed and equipped, landed in England, and in a bare six months were in the field holding their own line of trenches.

To appreciate the difficulties, however, that attended this transformation we must look back to those happy days prior to August, 1914, and witness the Canadian Militia in its own home.

This consisted of the "Drill-hall," or "Armouries," a long, low building equipped more or less with barred windows and castellated turrets at one or more corners. This building is one of the sights of the city, and is pointed out by the cabby or taxi-driver to the English gentlemen and other tourists who come out with the laudable intention of writing books.

If the castellated towers are missing, and the building is constructed on strictly utilitarian lines, one is safe in referring to it as the "Drill-hall"; but if a couple of old cannon, vintage 1800, guard its portals, and barred windows and frowning turrets add to its martial splendour, then you have an "Armouries." By observing this simple rule one can discriminate between the two as easily as telling a church from a cathedral.

The existence of such a building is largely due to the efforts of the local member of Parliament, and the style of architecture varies directly with the square of his popularity with the party in power. Thus a flourishing full-strength battalion may be housed in a dingy, drab wooden structure, and in the next town a very ornate and modern building may be tenanted by a corps that is only struggling for existence, or perhaps not even struggling. It is well, however, to refrain from too much criticism of these buildings, pretentious and hideous as they may be, for in them are taught the ideals and principles which so many of our youth have died to uphold in the rain-sodden fields of Flanders.

Considering the shortness of what is locally known as the "drill season," the results obtained are good. General French, in his report of a few years ago, described our horses as "half-broken and our men but little more," but that is only to be expected in a country where a man is considered to be wasting his time if he devotes even the little that he can ill afford to the military profession.

However, even if the half-broken men and horses do kick over the traces once in a while, they eventually "get there," and that, after all, is the Canadian doctrine.

For the purposes of training the Militia is divided into two classes—the "city" and the "rural" corps. There is also the permanent force, our Canadian regulars, who exist as a school for "the Militia," as they refer to the non-professional army.

The city corps consist chiefly of infantry, heavy artillery, and engineer corps, the last being generally in university towns and either affiliated with or being actually the cadet corps of the college. One might think the cadet corps would be affiliated with the Militia, but this is a case where the boy is father to the man.

City corps do fourteen nominal days' training a year in the drill-hall, and, of late years, a voluntary camp of five days. For each of these days two night drills of two hours each count as a day; the militiaman receives the sum of four shillings, with a slight increase according to his musketry ability.

The drill season commences in the middle of March, and from then on till Inspection Day—a boiling hot day in June—

the voice of the drill-sergeant is heard in the land. This individual is obtained on indent from the permanent force; but more of him anon.

For two nights a week, then, at the season when a young man's fancies are supposed to turn lightly to other things, the would-be Wellington dons a suit of rifle green, or scarlet, or even the heathen kilt, according to his taste, and, disguising it with a civilian great coat (regulation coats being issued to 50 per cent. of the establishment), slinks more or less bashfully down the back way to the drill-hall. There he will learn to shift a rifle (weight nine pounds five and a few odd ounces) from one position to another in response to quite unintelligible commands that echo most absurdly from the roof. He will also learn to move around the floor in something like the formations laid down in the little red manual, practising especially those for whom our prayers are desired, the favourites of the General Officer Commanding his district.

For, though regulations wax and wane, the G.O.C. changeth not; neither does he bow down and worship the little tin gods the Army Council set up. But instead, as one by one the formations he used to know are culled from the manual, he watches the new formations with a passive eye and reserves his choleric criticisms for the old reliables' "Echelon to the right" and that maximum of military perfection the "March Past."

In rural corps, however, the season consists of fourteen actual days spent in the broiling sun in camp. Lucky indeed is the company commander who can bring a full company every year to camp, for many who come one year come not again, and such are the conditions that no man sayeth him nay lest recruiting be stopped altogether in that district. One sighs for the press gang of Merrie England and subscribes for such incendiary journals as those of the various National Service Leagues, for one has a limited area to secure the recruits from, and must recruit at least 60 per cent. each year at a season when farm labour is at a premium.

Having secured your recruits, you must assemble them at some central point where you have a large quantity of arms and equipment stored, generally at your own expense—though "Sam" Hughes is remedying this—and issue these, stave off

15

complaints that the fit is not exactly up to West End standards, and, if you are an old "stager," give them an hour or two of drill while enthusiasm is at its maximum.

Then on the required date you marshal your little force at the railway station, shepherd them into the cars, and detrain them a few hours later, under even more trying circumstances, a few miles from camp. Then, with a mixture of patience, perspiration, and profanity, you finally march into your line of tents. Here you are met with great glee by the colonel and the adjutant, who inquire blithely as to how many men you have; this may seem useless, but as the men are strung out for at least half a mile along the route it is reassuring to learn how many there should be in the little procession.

We will take it that the colonel is pleased with your reply, in which case he will tell you that his white horse has arrived, so if you will drop around ... prohibition rules in our training camps, but a good O.C. has always something under the mat.

What follows in the remaining days of the fortnight must be endured to be appreciated. At the end of that time the shepherding begins again, and for the next month the company commander scours his district, this time locating uniforms which in defiance of his last orders, and prayers, have not been turned in. Very often the man has gone West and the uniform as well. So remote are the chances of seeing either again that the expression "Gone West" has almost the same meaning as the modern soldier's "Nah pooh!"

During the winter months classes of instruction are held in all the training centres, the instructors being the non-commissioned officers of the permanent Militia. The amount of good done depends largely on the ability and personal effort of the commanders of the local corps. During these months such officers as can spare the time or have not already done so become, by various long and tedious processes, involving much correspondence, attached to the various barracks for instruction.

This arrangement is a very popular one for all concerned, providing as it does—

1. Frequent leave for junior officers of the permanent force;

2. An opportunity to drill men who know, by years of experience, what movements one wishes to perform, and who will (D.V.) perform them with machinelike precision despite wrong commands;

3. A pleasant change in the ordinary drill for the above-mentioned men owing to the aforesaid wrong commands.

In the evenings lectures are given by senior officers who are not young, married, or talented in other ways. These lectures comprise the hundred and one things an officer is expected to know, from "Military Law" to "Protection when at Rest." This last subject will require revision after the present campaign, it being the writer's opinion that soldiers never rest—not when there is a foot of Allied soil unturned by a shovel, at any rate.

Eventually one passes an examination of sorts and becomes a qualified officer of Militia. The questions set are not hard—they would doubtless raise a smile if handed to a first year Sandhurst man—but they present real difficulties to officers whose opportunities are limited and whose spare time is largely taken up in the hard and thankless task of recruiting.

Officers of the permanent force are, in the main, graduates of the Royal Military College, Kingston, an institution second to none in the Empire. Field officers of Militia can also take a training course at the college, but the numbers who can avail themselves of this opportunity are limited.

Our staffs are assisted by very able officers loaned from the Imperial Army in exchange for officers of the same rank attached to Imperial battalions.

But the bulk of the instructional work is done, and exceedingly well done too, by the staff-sergeant—the Sergeant What's-'is-Name of Kipling's song.

He is very carefully selected and trained, and becomes in time a walking encyclopaedia of military affairs. He must be a marvel of tact and diplomacy as well, for not only will he meet the officer who knows nothing and appreciates that fact, but also that other type—not uncommon in civil life as well—the man who knows nothing yet thinks he knows all.

CHAPTER 2

Petewawa

Petewawa is the training ground of the Canadian Field Artillery and the Permanent Force. Until very recently it was strictly reserved for them, and was regarded, by those who had not been there, as a sort of seventh heaven for soldiers. Later, when the city corps were taken there for five days one June—or was it July?—we changed our minds and decided that, geographically speaking, it was part of one of Dante's seven circles. At present it is the internment camp for enemy aliens, and if they endure it for the duration of the war the Kaiser should present them, one and all, with iron crosses.

Fifty square miles of sandy hills, covered here and there with second growth scrub, it is an ideal ground for the purpose. The temperature rises to 98 deg. Fahrenheit most of the days in summer. What it is like in winter the writer does not know—probably 40 deg. below zero, as our climate does nothing by halves.

The name, curiously enough, means "a sound (or music) as of water falling in the distance." Anyone who has toiled through its sands in a July sun can appreciate the subtle humour of the red man who named it. Other attractions are sand fleas, mosquitoes, and black flies, so that after passing through a fortnight in Petewawa one is versed in all modern methods of warfare, including the subterranean and the aerial.

Here the artillery do all their training—heavy and fortress artillery excepted. The latter, however, send quotas each year, though performing their actual drill in their armouries. There are other artillery camps, but none of the importance of Petewawa, for it is essentially an active service camp. Jackets are strapped to the limbers, shirt sleeves rolled to the elbows, and straw hats, locally known as "cow-breakfasts," take the place of the more military cap. The gunner reverts to his original state and becomes a farmer again. And he is none the less a good gunner for so doing. Men who can understand the mechanism of a modern combined reaper and binder have no trouble learning the recoil apparatus of an eighteen-pounder gun, and for drivers one cannot find a better man than the farmer, for the man enlisting as such brings his own team with him and naturally will not neglect them.

So one sees the batteries drawn up behind cover, firing slowly and deliberately as they do now on a "quiet" day along the Western front.

A sharp report, a glint of flame and of the gun recoiling between the two men sitting on either side of the trail, and another shell is whirring on its way to the target. Almost before the recoil is finished the breech is opened and another round thrust in, and the breech closes with a *clitch-clatch* of its own. A few seconds later corrections come over the telephone and another shell goes speeding overhead.

With the infantry, however, Petewawa is a different matter. To them it means manoeuvres; and every soldier knows what manoeuvres mean. There is a popular idea that these tactical exercises are enjoyed by the officers. Perhaps they are, if perchance one is on the staff, a dizzy height the writer has not yet attained.

Let us follow the fortunes of a typical Militia battalion during the several days covered by this mysterious term "manoeuvres."

The General Idea has been received the night before and duly discussed at the "pow-wow" or conference that always follows the reception of this document. Much time and whisky has been consumed, and the sum of the evening's discussion is that the General Idea is exactly the same as last year's, with the exception that the Blue Force is fighting the Grey Force this year. "Last year we had the Red Army to contend with, and the fact that they no longer oppose us is due to the annihilation they suffered"—so says the colonel. "The invasion is coming from the north—presumably the Eskimo are up in arms against us."

Dawn brings with it reveille and brigade orders. This is a magnificent bluff on the part of the brigade staff to give the impression that they have sat up all night devising new and wondrous schemes for departing from the beaten path of military science. This is quite unnecessary, as sufficient departures will occur naturally in the course of the day, and nothing on earth will convince the infantry officer that the staff ever work.

The colonel, however, reads the orders to the little group around him. First there is the General Idea, laboriously copied from orders of the night before. Then comes the "Special Idea." This, too, bears a time-worn similarity to its predecessors, but passes without special comment. The next heading is "Dispositions": "The advanced guard will consist of one troop of the Missinabee Horse and one company of the Umpteenth Battalion." "Thank God for that!" murmurs the colonel, realising that the one company of his battalion will be spared the arduous duty of trying to replace cavalry, and that the other three will be in the first of the fray and consequently the first out of ammunition and free from the danger always incidental to the use of blank ammunition at close ranges. Moreover, advanced guards have always been his hobby, so he proceeds to issue his orders—verbally of course, though he will write them out later for the sake of curious generals who make collections of such things. While he is waiting for the cavalry to report he engages in very earnest conversation with Begbie Lyte, the signalling officer. Lyte is the serious-faced young man standing arguing with his little knot of flag-waggers. He has just realised that one mistake has already been made in the campaign, for, in the enthusiasm of youth, he brought bicycles to Petewawa. He realises, too, that next year he will either bring no bicycles or no men, for the latter having pushed their machines through three miles of sand from the detraining platform are already expressing their opinion, with true Canadian freedom, as to their usefulness.

This difficulty is tactfully overcome by leaving the cycles in the tents, and the "plot," as he calls the instructions he has just received, is unfolded to them.

Meanwhile the cavalry come up, and the officer-in-charge, knowing somebody who knows Lyte, spends a few seconds in the exchange of pleasantries. His name being Horace Smith, it has been quite conveniently shortened to "Horsey." Smith is one of those geniuses who knows everybody whom anyone knows; consequently he is always able to borrow money. Presently he trots off with his troop, and we know we shall see no more of him until nightfall. In our turn we move off as well, and the main body, already commencing to munch the haversack lunches they are carrying, cherish similar opinions as to our fate.

Eventually the whole column is moving down the dusty road and presently turns northward, following some wheel tracks that eventually merge into the sand. Then for a long time nothing happens. The cavalry have long since disappeared; the vanguard of one company shows up occasionally on a hill top ahead of us and proves that we are at least moving in the same general direction.

At one time two men detached themselves from the rest of the vanguard and proceeded to divest themselves calmly of their accoutrements. Then followed the feverish wagging of a flag in a manner that suggested news of greatest importance. The colonel becomes impatient as he waits for the message to come through, and suggests mildly that there seems to be a falling off from the standard rate.

Lyte, however, is equal to the occasion, and calls to the reading signallers "Tell the fool to semaphore!" "He carn't," gasps the sergeant in a horrified whisper; "He's young, an' he don't know nothink but Morse." Lyte groans. This young lad was pressed into service a few days previously, on the strength of his boy scout record, to fill a gap caused by another youth who had suddenly felt the call of the wild and gone river boating.

Eventually the message is received and the flags on the hill top disappear as the signallers hasten to catch up with their party. It is the type of message embraced under the heading "Negative Information" and stated to be of importance.

Scouts report no enemy in sight as yet, 10.15 a.m.
J. Horace Smith (Lieut.)

There is a feeling that we have been deceived, and we trudge on, kicking up angry little swirls of dust. Sympathy is already beginning to be expressed for the children of Israel in their wanderings. The music of water falling in the distance would be music indeed, for most of the water bottles are by now empty, and great beads of sweat are standing out on the men's foreheads as a result. Men will not learn that drinking large quantities of water when marching only increases their discomfort.

However, other things soon occur to divert our minds; one or two false alarms that the enemy has been sighted are satisfactorily straightened out, with more flag-wagging, and finally the plop-plop of blank cartridge is heard in the distance.

The advance guard now extends in long skirmishing lines with a view to brushing aside any slight resistance offered by the enemy. Presently we come on the horses of our mounted brethren in little groups of four in rear of a hill, and as we climb the hill itself we see the backs of Smith's gallant troopers as they fire from behind bushes that would certainly prove their death warrants on active service. The enemy are hidden in the edge of a large and straggly wood that only two days before was the scene of a roaring bush fire. Occasionally a man can be seen moving against the background of the charred trunks, but they, too, are making the best of what cover there is. Smith, leaving us to clear the wood, withdraws his men and reports to the colonel, and then moves around to a flank, hoping to cut off the party inside the wood.

Meanwhile the main guard have reinforced the first thin lines of skirmishers, and the enemy are already falling back through the wood. We follow at a more leisurely pace, as the whole place is a mass of charred tree trunks, burnt underbush and ashes. A voice from the rear bids us "Lie down" in no uncertain tones, so, reflecting that after all the Government knows best, we do so, and from then on the khaki begins to blend with its surroundings in a way that the inventor of this variety of cloth never dreamed of.

The wood turns out to be pear-shaped, and we, having by chance struck the small end of the pear, emerge considerably before the other battalions, who, having come up on our right, are biting into the largest part of the pear. Sounds of heavy conflict arise, and having still some five rounds each of blank we re-enter the wood and the combat. From then on, as Lyte expressed it afterwards, "Things began to occur just as they happened, like all great battles, the strategy being worked out later."

Twice we engage friendly battalions until stopped by an irate umpire, and once we surround and capture three sections of the enemy's horses. These are found in a little *coulee* running off a dried stream bed. Altogether it is a glorious affair, and is just settling down to the stage when personal combat begins when a bugle blares out the "Cease fire." This is followed by the "assembly," and we straggle to the edge of the wood to find most of our battalion there. The brigade is again formed up and we sit down for lunch. The cavalry, our enemies of the morning, trot back to camp, where a hot meal awaits them, and we know we shall not see them again. As we have our blankets following we wonder what is in the wind. We soon learn, however—the rest of the day is to be spent in a route march to Chalk River, a stream about ten miles further north, and bivouac will be made there. Blankets are to be worn *en banderole*.

The whole brigade busies itself in drawing the blankets from the wagons and rolling them into long cylinders, which with a spare boot-lace are made into an exaggerated sort of horse-collar. The luckless owner then thrusts a head and one arm through the roll and he is ready to move on. A hotter method of carrying a blanket could scarcely be devised, but it is much preferable to the antique leather equipment that hangs year in and year out on the armoury walls.

Presently the column moves off along the dusty road, a mere trail winding through the brush, which, pleasant and green at first, soon is as drab and sordid as the weltering men along the road. Now and again a halt is ordered, and we throw ourselves on the roadside while another battalion passes through to take its turn at the head of the column. Some artillery wagons pass at the trot, raising clouds of dust and profanity along the line, and then the piping of a whistle starts the whole column moving again.

Chalk River is eventually reached and the bivouac formed; then the joyful shout of "Tea up" is heard. Several buglers at the same time play the "Men's Mess Call" with variations, and for a while contentment reigns.

The officers stroll around to the Y.M.C.A. tent and write postcards home, telling blithely how they are enjoying the lovely weather—not a cloud in the sky! They mention nothing of the blistered necks and sunburned noses from which the skin is already peeling. Begbie Lyte, with a shameless disregard for the truth, buys a postcard of a typical bunch of troops passing up that very same road, and selecting a figure well concealed by dust, marks an X over it, and inscribing "This is me" on the reverse side addresses it to the colonel's daughter.

The cool of the evening soon drives the noisy bathers from the river, and the camp settles down around the inevitable camp fires until the warning notes of "Last Post" and "Lights Out" sound.

The moon comes out and shines on long rows of blanketed forms and stacked rifles, and the only sound is the uneasy stir of the horses and tossing of an occasional man where the sand flea is already at work.

Such is a typical day at Petewawa.

CHAPTER 3

Mobilisation

It required the outbreak of the war to bring home the inevitable weakness of such a system, and when the Canadian Parliament announced the intention of sending a contingent of thirty thousand men, even the most enthusiastic shrugged their shoulders and said "Impossible."

But the feat not only was accomplished, but nearly trebled in the accomplishment, and if there is one man who can claim to have arisen as a Moses from among the people and achieved this miracle it is Major-General Sir Sam Hughes, at that time known generally as Sam Hughes, the Minister of Militia.

Sam Hughes did not arise in a single hour—neither was Rome built in a day. He had been rising for several years, and it had taken the combined efforts of both the Liberal and the Conservative parties to hold him down.

Looking backward one cannot help thinking what a pity it was he had not been given a free hand. He supported the Ross rifle, and raised it from the status of a political weapon to that of a military one, and whatever opponents to this weapon may claim they must remember that it was the weapon that held the line at Ypres in those last few days of April, 1915, and had it not been available the Canadian Division would have probably been in England patiently drilling with dummy rifles, and the glory of having saved the situation would have fallen upon other troops.

However, the actual declaration of war drew people's attention to the Militia, and they demanded action.

Some commanding officers made stirring speeches by platform or Press, offering the services of their battalions as complete units—an impossibility to accomplish owing to the terms of enlistment; others with more modesty sent in their applications, without any flourish of trumpets, for service in any capacity.

But along the border, wherever there were canals, bridges, and other public works that might easily be damaged by fanatic sympathisers from the United States, volunteers were called for to supply the necessary guards.

Subsequent events justified these precautions, but for some time the men on duty were the object of much attention from the small boy and that type of young man who still roams the streets and declares that the Allies are a long time winning the war!

Spy fever was rampant, and such experts as Begbie Lyte were constantly in demand to investigate lights that flickered in any manner that a vivid imagination might possibly take for signalling.

At other points practical jokes were played, such as driving a calf at night in the direction of the sentry. The soldier receiving no answer to his challenge would fire in the direction of the noise, and a loud laugh would greet him. Once or twice, however, the sentry waited for the laugh and fired in that direction, so that this variety of joke soon lost its popularity.

Once, however, mobilisation had been ordered the militiamen were replaced by men who had volunteered for active service. The armouries began to hum with activity. In the West it was hard to find accommodation for the men who came from isolated homesteads and lonely ranches, some even from the Arctic Circle, to enlist. The West still continues to supply the bulk of our recruits, due largely to the fact that the majority are, if not British born, at least the sons of British fathers, and consequently felt the call more personally than the sons of families four or five generations in the country. Quebec, from which province one would expect the most owing to the ties of race and language with our Allies, has been frankly disappointing, although certain exclusively French-Canadian battalions have done, and are continuing to do, as good work as any on the Western front.

A week or two dragged on before the actual order to depart

for the big concentration camps came, and various conjectures were made as to their location. Petewawa was suggested as one, but given up as too isolated. Niagara, Barriefield, Three Rivers, and other "annual" sites were other favourites, but each had some objection, for no concentration such as thirty thousand men had been held in the history of Canada.

Eventually, however, we learned that one large camp was to be formed at Val Cartier. Except that Val Cartier was in Quebec, no one knew anything of this little hamlet.

Orders came thick and fast ordering this equipment to be worn and that to be left behind. Some days rifles were to be taken and greatcoats left in stores, and next day the rifles were to be left and greatcoats were to be taken. The result was that some of the telegrams went astray, and commanding officers at the last minute ordered what equipment they thought most suitable to be worn.

The Umpteenth Battalion took down the leather harness that had adorned its armoury walls for many a year and spent an anxious day fitting it together, Begbie Lyte and the other officers who had volunteered for the front flitting from one group of contestants to another.

At last every man had a working knowledge of the fifty odd buckles and a hazy idea as to where the straps were supposed to cross his chest and where not. The colonel looked with pride on this difficulty overcome and said, "Thank Heaven! we will probably get a more modern outfit as soon as we strike camp." Alas! We buckled and unbuckled those straps and rolled and unrolled our greatcoats for half a year before the new kit was handed out.

This was only one of the many steps that led up to that final day when, with the band playing such cheerful airs as "The Girl I left behind me" and "Will ye no come back again," the active service volunteers of the Umpteenth Battalion left their native town.

The way to the station is but dimly remembered as a haze of faces, spasmodic attempts at cheering, and the waving of many handkerchiefs. Much handshaking and the sudden thrusting of presents into arms already full prefaced the actual pulling out of the train.

The officers gathered on the back of the last car and watched the white faces of the crowd dwindle to pin points, and then a curve hid town and people alike from view.

It was less lonely inside the car, where were officers of another battalion whose men were in the fore part of the train. The elder men talked in low, serious tones as befitted those who knew something of what lay before them.

To Lyte and the younger subalterns it seemed as though they were on the threshold of life's Great Adventure, as indeed they were.

But they were not facing a war of chivalrous deeds such as they imagined.

Alas for our ideals! war now appears in its true light, as the game of commerce played on a larger scale with human lives as pawns in the place of dollars and cents!

And as for chivalry, how can it live in the midst of machine-guns, asphyxiating gases, and liquid flames?

CHAPTER 4

Val Cartier

A more picturesque site for a camp than Val Cartier could hardly be imagined, situated as it was among the foothills of the Laurentian mountains along the banks of the Jacques Cartier River.

A gentle slope, dry sandy soil, and plenty of water made it ideal from a sanitary standpoint, and with the ample manoeuvre grounds available, the shower sprays, and running water piped throughout the camp, Val Cartier was the peer of any camp the Canadians have yet seen.

But when we tumbled out of the train in the early morning there was nothing to show the existence of a military camp except one lonely bell-tent guarding the railway platform and a pair of wheel-tracks disappearing in the clumps of second-growth cedars.

Following these tracks we came upon an opening on either side of the road in which men laboured at clearing away the underbrush. The vivid colours of the jerseys in which they were clad told the world that those on the one side were students from McGill, while those on the other clad in blue and white represented 'Varsity (Toronto). Further along the red, yellow, and blue of Queen's University showed where their University Field Company was at work. The same spirit of competition that existed on the football field now kept the three units working at top speed.

A patch of land that one day was covered with cedars would next day be bare of all but stumps, the brushwood blazing mer-

29

rily in huge fires. Next day the stumps in turn would be gone and by evening the new area would be covered with tents.

Already some hundreds of tents had been erected on each side of what was to be the main street of the camp. A ditching machine pantingly laboured on one side of the road and dug as much in a day as fifty men. In the ditch already made on the other side pipes had been laid and running water was available.

Showers had been erected for each company, and, most welcome of all, the advance party greeted us with a flourish of dirty aprons and ladles and the joyful cry of "skillet."

During the afternoon greatcoats were received, and very necessary they were, for when we rose next morning ice had formed in our pails, and the trees on the mountain side were beginning to turn red.

Long before we left the mountain sides were a wild revel of colour, reds, yellows, and browns predominating, where the frost had touched the leaves. Particularly brilliant were the shot-scarred trees that stood on the slopes forming the stop-butts of the rifle-ranges.

These ranges are worthy of special mention, comprising as they did targets for fifteen hundred men.

The method of construction was simplicity itself. A deep ditch had been dug and the earth thrown up like an ordinary trench to protect the marker. Strong posts had been erected about six feet apart to carry the targets, which took the form of squares of pulp-board mounted on a lever pivoted to the upright. The weight of the target held it behind the butt, and it was brought into view by pulling a short piece of rope attached to the free end of the lever.

Crude as this arrangement was, it served the purpose admirably, and daily we trudged out toward the mountain, around the foot of which this trench wound much as the German line does around the foot of Messines Hill, and fired ragged volleys into the re-echoing hill sides.

In only two ways could the training have been improved, and neither of these two was practicable under the circumstances.

Better checking of the target registers and fire control would have necessitated officers trained better in musketry, and such officers were not available, and had the latest pattern ammunition in clips been obtainable instead of the old square-toed bullet wrapped in paper packages, more practice in rapid fire—the English Army's Mad Minute—could have been had.

But Sam Hughes had to work with the material at hand, and from an army of men who had, in the majority, never fired a service rifle in their lives, he formed an army that he described as being "the finest shooting army in the world."

Drill was not by any means neglected, and there were few idle hours in camp, even moonlight nights being eagerly seized upon by battalion commanders for extra work.

Daily fresh drafts from battalions arrived and were formed into new composite battalions, and daily the proportion of men in old civilian clothing grew less.

Two reviews were held, after one of which the Honourable Sam had many things to say to the officers. He told them that every officer, no matter what political gender, would have an equal chance in the great struggle for a place on the contingent, for instead of the one thousand officers asked for some fifteen hundred officers were actually in camp.

Sam spake yet other homilies to the officers, and his address, delivered from a mound on which he and his staff were drawn up, was irreverently referred to around camp as the "Sermon on the Mount." A story is also told that one of his aides suggested that all could not hear him. "That's all right," he is credited with replying; "they can all see me!"

However, his words had a beneficial effect on all who heard them, and when two weeks later another review was held and His Royal Highness the Duke of Connaught inspected the contingent it was announced that the First Canadian Division was ready to proceed over seas.

Begbie Lyte and other signalling officers were summoned over to headquarters one day and received mysterious instructions from an officer in naval uniform.

Two days later, on the 22nd of September, the—Battalion

embarked on a troopship, and after a wild evening's pleasure at the Chateau Frontenac the writer, Begbie Lyte, and some others sought the narrow confines of the ship. The rhythmic throb of the propeller woke them some hours later as the ship moved out to anchor in mid stream.

CHAPTER 5

The Convoy

For two days we lay at anchor opposite the Citadel of Quebec and bemoaned the fate that separated us from the twinkling lights of the Chateau Frontenac and the Dufferin Terrace. Then one evening the throb of the propeller drew the crowd from the saloons to the decks and we watched the lights fade away in the night. From the forts long fingers of light followed us down stream, and blinking lights here and there sent us farewell greetings. Up on the bridge we could hear the clatter of the signal lamps, and the sooty odour of petroleum smoke hung in the calm air around us. Begbie Lyte was on the job and became an important unit in our little company. Through him alone would we get news of the outside world for some weeks to come.

Nearing Father Point, below Quebec, where normally the pilot is dropped or taken on when one is leaving or proceeding to Canada, the ship's officers pointed out a small twinkling light that marked the grave of the ill-fated *Empress of Ireland*. We had seen the collier *Storstadt* that sent her to her doom while at anchor off the Citadel, and were much impressed.

As night wore on the groups on the deck became smaller until the ship's officers alone remained, and with darkened portholes we slipped on through the night. A distinct freshness in the wind spoke of a change around us. We were nearing salt water. Next day we anchored in Gaspe Basin. Already some six or eight ships lay there.

There we lay for some days watching the jellyfish and the gulls while one by one our number was increased to thirty-two.

At this point a diversion occurred in the form of the last visit by the Minister of Militia in a noisy tugboat. More important than the printed copies of his farewell speech that were handed us was the news that now was our last chance to mail letters. In childish simplicity we handed down our mail, thinking the "hame folk" would receive these in a few short days. The sacks were collected and taken to one of the other ships and journeyed across the Atlantic with us. So our departure was kept secret from all but a few, for, with a shrewd knowledge of the "habitant" mind, Captain Gee, the gallant commander of "E" Company, tied up a few letters in a handkerchief, weighted it with sundry pieces of silver, and dropped the package into a fishing boat that had come alongside with a load of fresh meat. The very amount enclosed spoke of secrecy, and the "habitant" sailor used all due precautions in forwarding the missives.

By Sunday noon the ground swell had driven some of the officers to deck chairs, while the others marshalled the troops on the rear deck for Divine service. Service over, we watched the celebrated Perce Rock fading in the distance and knew that Canada now lay far behind us. A day later and Newfoundland too lay in the distance, and the magic circle of the horizon closed around us.

Interest now began to be taken in things nautical. The sextant, compass, and log were the cause of much discussion, and the usual bets were made on the daily run, the stakes being held by the chaplain.

Three days out and the ship's library was taken by assault, and the sevenpenny novels that formed it disappeared into the cabins. In vain an officer was appointed librarian with powers to search and to seize, but conditions were not bettered.

Lectures, physical drill, and other mild duties relieved a little of the monotony, for the journey was a slow one, a condition made necessary by the horse transports, one of which rolled in line ahead of us. Occasionally a stir would be noticed on her decks and a horse that had succumbed to *mal-de-mer* would be unceremoniously dumped overboard. Such occasions were marked by a fusillade of pistol shots from each ship as the car-

Sailing down the St. Lawrence, near Bic

case drifted past, for, contrary to traditions, most of us carried revolvers for the first time in our lives and were anxious to display our prowess.

Nearly a fortnight was thus passed gazing in singular apathy at the most remarkable demonstration of the command of the seas that military history of any age affords.

In three long lines, roughly a mile apart, the transports formed an armada such as Philip of Spain never dreamed of.

But about two days out from England a black column of smoke was seen to port, and presently the contour of a heavy battleship could be determined bearing down on us. There was wild excitement till the Cross of St. George could be distinguished at her masthead. It was the ill-fated *Queen Mary*, our latest and finest battle-cruiser. At an almost incredible speed she overtook us and passed up our lines with her crew manning the decks and her band playing The *Maple Leaf*.

From then on we always could see the smoke of heavier battleships in the offing, and knew we were getting close to somewhere.

We passed the Scilly Islands about 4 o'clock in the morning, but as cards had continued till late the preceding night few but the ship's officers saw the pin-point of light marking the westward sentinel of the Old World.

Then on October 14th fishing smacks again appeared and the grey coast of Cornwall hove in sight, and by noon we could distinguish buildings along the cliffs.

Passing the Eddystone our course was altered and all hopes of landing at Southampton vanished. Captain H—r was much excited. After nineteen years he was returning to his native town—Plymouth. To a running fire of his explanations we passed up the Sound to the Hamoaze. A tugboat, looking ridiculously small against the gigantic liner ahead, now took us in tow, and the throbbing of the ship's screw stopped. The cessation of this pulse added a sombre touch to our voices; we were nearing the end of the voyage, and in another day would know the ship no more.

Thus we glided slowly past the old wooden cruisers now used as training ships, and from their crowded riggings came

Church parade

shrill treble cheers. To the piping of the young cadets' voices was added the screaming of sirens and the tooting of many whistles. Halyards on all sides of us broke out into brilliant bunting and semaphores wagged with a madness that even Lyte could not translate.

The clarion notes of the mess bugle called us from the decks to other duties, and there between the soup and the fish we heard the hoarse rattle of the anchor chain as we found our moorings.

Captain H—r, seizing the opportunity, rose, and in the capacity of an old Plymothian gave us greeting.

Such was our welcome to England.

In the morning we looked out and saw rows and rows of chimney pots, impressive in their similarity.

Then later we read an editorial in *The Times* describing us as pioneers and backwoodsmen. This provoked much comment, but the writer for one was not greatly distressed, for he had been born within sound of the shrill of a sawmill, and the perfume of cedar is still sweeter to his nostrils than the costly unguents of Araby.

CHAPTER 6

In England

Our stay in England was marred by the heaviest rainfall of many years, and Salisbury Plain, where we were quartered all winter, had the reputation of being the muddiest spot in the world until we struck Flanders; and even now there are patriots who maintain that the "Plain" holds the championship.

But these were not our first impressions of the Downs. It is hard yet to reconcile the mud in which we lived for months with the velvety swards that first greeted our eyes.

We had detrained at Amesbury, bleary eyed and sleepless after a tedious night trip from Plymouth. This had followed a seemingly interminable march through Plymouth, during which our progress had been seriously delayed by women who broke into the ranks and kissed and wept over our dear boys. Officers escaped with mere handshakes, but still found the ordeal rather trying.

However, a few minutes of standing around the platform munching sandwiches while the necessary mistakes were made and corrected wakened us thoroughly, and then to the crunch of our own footsteps we swung smartly down the village street.

Here we found we were in a new world, a world we had read of in books. The thatched cottages, the neatly-clipped hedges, the churchyard with its headstones and tumbling wall, all seemed to fit in with what we expected. When we passed a public-house with its wooden sign emblazoned with "The Three Feathers," or some such emblem, the picture was complete—it was the England of Jeffery Farnol!

Eastern Ontario Regiment, near Stonehenge

Later we swung across the ample Downs, passing on our way Stonehenge. After having said "I don't know" to a few hundred questions from the men nearest you, it was a relief to be able to answer a few for a change. What memory failed to supply imagination furnished; but this is every guide's privilege. A momentary halt here—to give the men a rest—afforded a chance for cameras to click, and then we left the road and marched across the grassy Downs to the Bustard Inn. Here the rows of tents that were to be our homes for the next few months had already been pitched.

Other brigades went to Lark Hill, to Pond Farm, to Sling Plantation, and to West Down, North and West Down, South ... one could lose a whole army in this vast training ground.

Gone was the long main street of Val Cartier camp with its cinema shows and booths of tempting merchandise. Gone, too, was the little river with its gravelly shores for bathing.

But we were one step nearer our goal, and that was the one thought that consoled us during those trying winter months that followed. From then on we saw little but our own brigade—the 1st Brigade—and the Princess Patricia's Light Infantry—who were also at Bustard Camp.

The latter held themselves rather aloof from the Canadian Division, counting themselves as superior troops—as indeed they were, being mostly veterans of one or two campaigns—and as they were not brigaded with us we saw little of them.

Early in November the King, accompanied by Lords Roberts and Kitchener, reviewed the Division. His Majesty took special interest in the Patricias, so we were not surprised when in the early days of December the "Pats" left the Plain to join the 27th Division. Of their subsequent doings another book might be written, for no regular battalion of the British Army has proved itself steadier on the field than this magnificent corps—the gift to the Empire of a very gallant gentleman who has since succumbed to wounds received while serving with it in the field.[1]

---

1. Major Hamilton Gault, referred to above, did not die of wounds as first reported, but suffered the loss of a leg by amputation.

MANOEUVRES ON SALISBURY PLAIN

Christmas brought with it leave and relaxation from the monotony of drilling, but with the New Year we started brigade and divisional manoeuvres, and we knew our stay on the Plain was drawing to a close.

We were again reviewed—in a drizzling rain this time—by the King on February 4th, 1915, and on the following day—just six months after the declaration of war—the First Canadian Division, complete in every detail (horse, foot, and guns) entrained for France.

So secret had the departure been kept that people in the neighbouring town of Salisbury knew nothing of the review or the entraining of the troops till they were well on the high seas.

After a very rough passage from Avonmouth the Division landed at St. Nazaire in the Bay of Biscay, the last transport arriving some time in the second week of February.

From there they were taken in box cars to that mysterious region known as "the front," travelling forty men or eight horses to a car, a state of affairs that one man complained "showed undue regard for horses."

But five whole battalions and a number of surplus officers who had managed to get over to England supernumerary to their battalions were left behind on the Plain as a base depot.

Amongst the latter were the writer and Begbie Lyte, and when they rejoined a month or two later their battalion had been cut to pieces and some twenty-five of the officers with whom they had trained were casualties.

It is hard to imagine anything sadder than rejoining a battalion after fighting such as that unless it is the saying of good-bye.

CHAPTER 7

Interim

For a time there was little news from the Canadians at the front, for they were not immediately placed in the trenches. Trench warfare was then still a novelty; its exact principles had not been developed, and all the training done on the Plain had been the ordinary open style of fighting—quite useless against the strongly entrenched positions the Germans had taken up.

So while lying in reserve behind the lines the First Division dug and manned trenches and practised themselves in the new warfare. Selected officers from each company spent days in the front line with other battalions and returned to their men bristling with information.

A little later selected platoons and companies took their turn in the front line, and before the end of February the Canadian Division was holding its own sector of the British line. Casualties began to drift back to the Canadian base, which had now become centred at Shorncliffe, and letters began to arrive with details of the new methods of fighting. There was other news, too, of a more cheerful sort that showed brighter glimpses of life that occurred when enjoying brief rests from the firing line.

"Don't sympathise with us too much," wrote one officer; "we would sooner be here than on the Plain. Last night we gave an oyster and champagne supper at—to three Ottawa ladies who are running a soup and coffee wagon for our battalion. We had a great time. D— Dang and the Cat (another subaltern) were in fine fettle."

But more serious work was in view.

On March 10th the British commenced an offensive at Neuve Chapelle which, had it proved successful, would have involved the Canadians in the projected advance upon the Aubers Ridge, which formed the key to Lille.

But Neuve Chapelle, although a victory in one sense of the word, was a very costly lesson, but a lesson that showed that our artillery must be enormously increased if any further effort to break through the German line was to be made.

For, having taken their objective, the British troops found not only a second but a third line of trenches protected by entanglements of a most formidable nature, and so situated as to render the ground recently won at such heavy cost almost untenable. To carry these lines would require another bombardment more intense even than that which had preceded the attack. Our line had advanced one mile and there it stayed.

So ended the first attempt on our part to renew the offensive after the stagnation of a winter of trench warfare. For years we had been taught that an army that relinquishes the offensive acknowledges itself as beaten. It now began to look as though military science had undergone a complete revolution and that trench warfare and the policy of attrition were to be the normal methods of the future.

But Neuve Chapelle showed something else—it showed that the indomitable spirit of our men had not been quenched by the misery and suffering of the winter months and that the British bayonet was as much to be feared as ever.

"We were kept pretty busy," wrote a friend, "doing rapid fire, and lost quite a few from shell fire. But our artillery had the time of their lives, and fired pretty steadily the whole three days of the show."

Later he wrote that they were moving northward—probably to Hill 60—and we could expect there would be something doing shortly.

It was not to Hill 60 that the Canadian Division went, but further northward in the Ypres salient to the left of the 27th Division, where the "Princess Pats" were winning immortality at St. Eloi.

So the days wore on, the surplus officers chafing at the monotony of drill on a barrack square, relieved as it was by "Thes Dansants" at the Metropole and promenades along the Leas at Folkestone.

Then one day a medical officer dropped a sure tip. He had been warned to prepare beds for a thousand casualties—the Canadians were in something big at last!

Just how big it was we realised a week later when the newspapers broke forth into flamboyant headlines:

Canadians Saved Situation
Four Guns Recaptured

and other startling sentences that danced before the eyes.

Lyte and the writer were returning from some light festivities, when the hoarse cry "All about the Canadians" arrested their attention. Papers were hurriedly bought, and the brief vague lines of the official *communique* eagerly scanned. "By Jove!" was Lyte's exclamation; "but isn't that great!" The writer, however, hardly heard him; he was thinking of the many good friends who had taken part and the price they had to pay, and his answer was the monosyllabic "Huh!" of the aborigine.

That evening we packed our kits.

CHAPTER 8

Ypres, 1915

The Second Battle for Ypres, as the fighting at Langemarck and St. Julien is officially designated, was largely a regimental and company officers' battle. This does not, however, reflect adversely on the brigade and other staffs, who did all that was humanly possible with the information that was at hand. Even at this date there are questions about the action that cannot be cleared up until it will be permissible to reproduce the whole of the war diaries of the various units that took part.

On the 2nd and 3rd Canadian Brigades fell the brunt of the fighting in which the Canadians took part, as the 1st Brigade was in rest billets in reserve.

But, without detracting from their work, it must be admitted that the account by the official "Eye Witness" does not give the 1st Brigade the credit it deserves. This, however, is inevitable. In a modern battle one sees nothing but what happens in the immediate vicinity of the observer, and we must therefore depend largely on the accounts furnished by others of what occurred in other parts of the field.

It will do no harm, however, to quote from the description by an officer, since killed, of the action of one of the battalions of this brigade, which from respect for the censor must remain nameless. It would, however, serve no purpose to conceal the true names of those officers and men whom he thought fit to mention, for the majority of them have also laid down their lives in the field.

During the latter part of the evening of April 22nd

French and Algerian troops in large numbers began re-
treating through *Vlamertinghe* in the utmost confusion,
throwing away their arms and crying *'Asphyxie! Asphyxie!!'*
Empty limbers and gun teams without their guns dashed
down the road, already thick with refugees and fugitive
soldiers. Captain Culling therefore ordered the company
to stand to arms and be ready to move off as soon as orders
were received.

Orders came about 9 p.m., and we moved off to the
battalion rendezvous at the junction of the Brielen road,
where we found the rest of the battalion formed up. From
here we continued north easterly up the Brielen road,
across the canal toward St. Julien.

A short distance past the canal the battalion deployed
from the road, No. 3 Company being on our (No. 2 Company's) left and continued to advance.

Moving forward in this formation was very difficult owing to the thick darkness and the ground being so cut up by
hedges, but Captain Culling got in touch with the battalion
on our left, which turned out to be the Canadian Scottish
under Lieutenant-Colonel Leckie, at about the farmhouse
that afterwards became our dressing station. The advance
continued slightly more to the north, and a few minutes
later the company lay deployed about fifty yards in rear of
a trench (A B) occupied by the 10th Canadian Battalion.
They were enfiladed from a German trench to their right
rear (C) and an adjoining farmhouse (M G).

Wounded men, including their commanding officer, Lieutenant-Colonel Boyle, lay everywhere about the
trench and *parados*, but they were too weak to attack this
short piece of trench, although it was rendering their position quite untenable.

One of our platoons successfully attacked this trench,
while another under Mr. Doxsee attacked the neighbouring house and succeeded in driving the enemy from it
with a loss of only two men killed and another wounded.

Steps were then taken to improve the position by re-

GERMAN LINE

WOOD

MG. HOUSE

DRESSING STA

BATT H.Q.

To ST JEAN

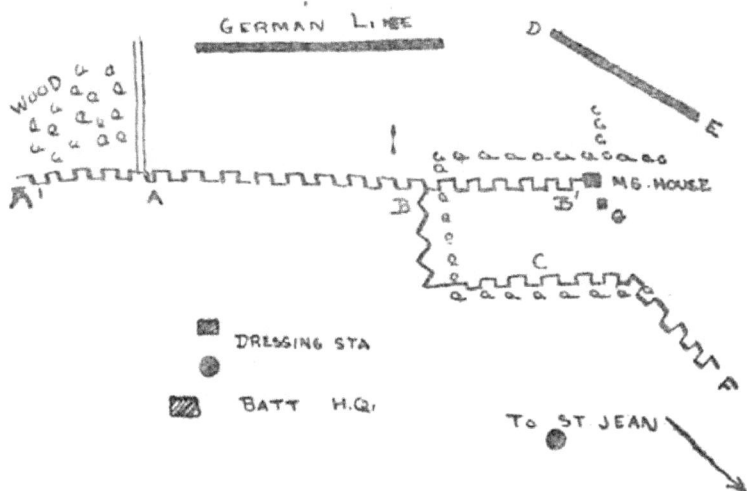

versing the parapet of the captured trench (C) and extending the original trench to the right. The house (M G), too, was prepared for defence, and thus the night was passed and no man slept.

At dawn of the 23rd the enemy commenced shelling the house and trench, but the losses inflicted were slight owing to the two parallel hedges, which made both ranging and observing difficult. They then commenced an attack on the house supported by machine-gun fire, which proved a far more serious affair, as in the house itself we lost two men killed and some wounded, while in the trench we lost two valuable men, Platoon-Sergeant Abelarde and Lance-Corporal McGurk. The former had crawled out along the hedge to a dangerous and commanding knoll, and from there put eighteen of the enemy out of action before a sniper's bullet found him. The dead lay exposed where they fell, and could readily be counted from the house.

About 9 o'clock, while Captain Culling was organising a counter-attack on a small portion of the German trench (D E), two companies of the Toronto Battalion under a major arrived as reinforcements, and took cover behind our *parados* as there was no room in the trench. Captain Culling asked that they take on the attack, and Mr. Doxsee volunteered to lead it. The response was feeble, and the attack petered out to nothing, Bugler Hunt and a man of the Toronto Battalion being killed by the side of Doxsee, who, finding himself alone, returned to the trench unharmed.

The Toronto men now tried a flanking movement on our immediate right, but lost eight men and had to abandon the attempt. However, coupled with our fire from the second story of the house, the effect was sufficient to cause the enemy to retire from this point, and the remainder of the day passed quietly, though the enemy's artillery continued to shell our position and a machine-gun played on the house at every sign of movement. By evening we had some seventeen casualties, a remarkably small number considering the shelling.

As soon as darkness set in, under cover of a few skirmishers, two platoons continued our original trench (A B) along a line (B B 1) about fifteen feet in rear of the forward hedge surrounding the house and linked this trench to the position in our right rear with a communication trench, the majority of this work being done with the small entrenching tool.

This enabled us to get the whole company under cover, and with a machine-gun of the 10th Battalion in the house we felt fairly secure. Captain Hooper held a house immediately in front of our lines called Hooper House, and our original trench was held by a mixture of our own men and the Canadian Scottish under Mr. Hugill.

Dawn on Saturday found our positions unaltered, but about 7 o'clock orders came from Lieutenant-Colonel Rodgers, our second in command, to take over all of the original trench and relieve the Scottish.

. Simultaneously Mr. Doxsee called for reinforcements to repel a direct frontal attack on our forward trench and machine-gun house.

Reinforcements hurried up along the new communication trench, but were anticipated by Mr. Scott and a score or so of men, who dashed across the open and repelled the attack, Mr. Doxsee being unfortunately killed at this point.

Captain Richardson now took over machine-gun house, and his company (No. 2) relieved us along our original trench. The two Toronto companies had entrenched to our right, forming a narrow and very dangerous salient (C F).

All day this house was the target of the enemy's artillery and machine-guns, the latter sweeping the building so effectively that the garrison was forced to lie flat on the floors.

Six attacks were made by their infantry and repulsed before they could get closer than two hundred yards, in spite of the fact that our only machine-gun jammed incessantly owing to the rapidity of its firing. About 2 p.m. one of our own guns came up, and from then on both guns remained in action.

About this time troops in French uniforms were seen moving down a road on our right toward St. Julien. At first no notice was taken of them, but presently it became apparent that these were Germans, who had adopted this ruse to get behind our flank.

Fire was immediately opened on them with what rifles could be spared from our front line, and one machine-gun was hastily posted in a barn (G), from which it did excellent work.

At 3.30 orders were received to retire in the direction of battalion headquarters. (These orders had originally been sent out at 2 o'clock, and when Lieutenant-Colonel Watson received no response he sent them again and again until he finally saw the last company passing the shattered house that had served alike as dressing station and battalion headquarters, and not till then did he leave the field himself.)

The retirement took place across open ground swept by both shrapnel and machine-guns, and the men just seemed to melt away.

Men straggled in for hours, and when the battalion

finally assembled at brigade headquarters at St. Jean the company had lost one hundred and thirty-nine of all ranks, of which four were officers.

It was a black situation. No one knew how other parts of the field had fared or how much ground had been lost. British troops were being rushed up to relieve the 2nd and 3rd Brigades, who in some incredible manner still held on in spite of two attacks with the gas. But they had paid a terrible price. Of the former brigade there were scarcely a thousand men and of the latter not many more.

If this, then, is the account of what one battalion—nay, what one or two companies—accomplished, what must be the stories, as yet untold, of those other battalions of the First Canadian Division that filled the gap that led to Calais?

CHAPTER 9

With the Draft

On returning to our barracks we found notices that "the following officers will hold themselves in readiness to proceed to their respective units with the next draft." Eagerly we scanned the list to make sure our names had not been omitted, and then transferred ourselves from the crowd that gathered in the ante-room to those who waited their turn outside the telephone cabinet. Letters and telegrams were being feverishly written in all parts of the building, and a hurly-burly of voices in the mess-room proclaimed the general opinion that we had been pretty badly cut up. A tailor's agent had somehow made his way into that sanctuary, and voices were demanding "Who can lend me a blank cheque?" in a wild endeavour to get him out again.

Telegrams were also arriving, one or two from the front. A subaltern spread the sheet of flimsy in his hand to find his cousin had been killed in action. There was a sudden hush in the turmoil as he turned and walked slowly to the window; men at such times are mute and trust to the simple pressure of the hand to tell that sympathy which the tongue cannot frame.

A colonel whose hair had grown grey in the service passed from one group to another, giving a word of advice here and receiving a word of sympathy there, for his age had debarred any further activities in the field. "But I have one son over there now," he proudly told you, "and my other is coming with the next contingent!"

The orderly room clerk entered and pinned up the daily orders. These were at once surrounded, and would have perished in the *melee* had the colonel not taken the situation in hand and read them out in his sternest parade voice with appropriate comments of his own.

"All officers and men warned for draft will parade to the ranges at 5 o'clock tomorrow morning—that will teach you to sit up all night playing cards!

"Markers and other details—that includes you, Lyte—will be at the butts and all targets ready for firing at a quarter before the hour, &c., &c.

"Light marching order will be worn by all ranks, including one hundred and fifty rounds per man. Haversack rations to be carried.

"Officers' valises—maximum weight thirty-five pounds—to be rolled ready for transport by 2 p.m., &c., &c."

This last caused an immediate thinning of the crowd, and till late that night we struggled over our kits, rolling and unrolling them to try and bring their weight down to something like the regulation amount.

At 4 o'clock next morning we fell in to march to the ranges, Lyte and his ill-fated companions having left half an hour before, and from then on till the afternoon we toiled in the hot sun. Returning about 3 that afternoon, we found the draft ordered to be ready to proceed at 6 o'clock, barely time for the men to get their tea; and tea in the Army is a meagre meal at the best of times.

Then after some hours waiting on the barrack square the draft moved off down the Cheriton road and through the streets of Folkestone to where the transports lay awaiting us.

Here the British Navy took hold of us again, and there were no further delays. The men were led below decks and packed as close as they could stand to one another, the officers having the privilege of being able to sit on their valises, which were piled unceremoniously on the deck.

Then when all were accounted for the mooring ropes were cast off, and with no more ceremony than the tinkle of the ship's telegraph we slid out of the harbour under cover of the scudding clouds.

But we were not alone. A long, lithe shape, strangely suggestive of a greyhound, crept out of the darkness around us and came up alongside, and a brief conversation, ending in "All right, full speed," was held.

The telegraph tinkled again and our ship bounded forward, leaving a long trail of phosphorescent foam in her wake.

The sighing of the rigging in the wind, the slap-slap of the Channel breakers at our sides, and the lashing *hish* of the spray across the decks blended with, but did not break, our thoughts.

And the dark shapes of the destroyers and the other transports momentarily revealed by gaps in the scudding clouds, the gleaming wake of the ship, and the faint white of the life-belts, that showed dimly where little groups of two or three stood or sat together, made a fitting scene for such an orchestral accompaniment.

Thus we reached France.

There followed a long march through the darkened streets of Boulogne to a camp on the Plains of St. Martin, not far from the tall column that marks where Napoleon gathered his great army and waited for the time that never came, when he would be master of that little strip of water we had just crossed.

A drizzling rain had started, and the men had now been nearly eight hours without food and practically a whole day without a proper meal. We were able to draw bully beef and biscuit at once from the stores, but the situation was really saved by the ladies at the Y.M.C.A. tent, who supplied hot cocoa and cake to all who cared to apply. A nominal charge of one penny was made to those who wished to pay, but no man was refused because of his inability to find this sum, small as it was.

Only a small thing, you may think, but it is only the smallest part of what this wonderful organisation is doing for the soldier at the front.

And a smile and a cup of coffee at 5 o'clock in the morning "look pretty good to me," as one recipient expressed it.

We were held in camp all the following day and then, carrying two days' rations, we entrained for the north. For a while we made vain attempts to find our destination from the French railway staff, but concluded they either did not understand our variation of their beautiful language or were sullen brutes knowing nothing.

As we continued northward the throbbing of distant gunfire became plainer, and a strange flickering could be seen in the morning sky. This strange light, caused by the flash of the guns and the flares or illuminating fuzees shot up by the infantry, resembled nothing so much as our own Aurora Borealis, and we were not surprised to find, a little later, that our men had already nicknamed them the "Northern Lights."

Dawn brought us to a halt by some little town where the engine-driver proceeded leisurely to fill his boiler. We availed ourselves of the chance to exercise our French on some Algerian troops who were lying wounded all over the platform. A rough tent had been made with wagon tarpaulins, and under this lay the worst cases—ghastly wrecks of men with blood-soaked bandages and blood-encrusted clothing, face muscles twitching convulsively as masses of flies settled on them. One French medical orderly with a strip of silver on his sleeves and an assistant seemed to be the whole staff of the place.

One tall chap with a handsome beard showed us how a bullet had torn through his cap and grazed his head, while a rude sling and a crutch spoke of a more serious injury of which he said nothing. His white teeth and smiling face turned to a horrible scowl as he continued talking, and thinking we were over-exciting him, we moved away. Had we only known, he was trying to describe to us the terrible effect of the asphyxiating gas on his comrades who were less educated than he!

A few miles further on we detrained at Poperinghe and were soon marching along a beautiful avenue of poplars—now perhaps the most famous highway in Flanders, the Vlamertinghe road.

Refugees passed us with all their worldly effects piled on a wagon, the women and little children clattering along behind in their wooden sabots. It seemed so unnecessary. The guns that had been pounding away all night were now strangely silent, and the fields on either side seemed peaceful enough. There was even a farmer ploughing stoically in one.

A little further on we saw a horse that had been hurriedly cut out from a gun or wagon team. It needed but one glance to tell us that shrapnel had done its deadly work there, and we wondered vaguely what had become of its rider, for the saddlery and harness were still on it.

On entering Vlamertinghe we saw signs of shelling on most of the buildings, particularly around the church and the square, the steeple of the former forming, of course, the aiming mark for the German guns. Here, too, the body of a woman lay half in and half out of a doorway. The place seemed absolutely deserted. An aeroplane droned overhead, but whether our own or the enemy's we could not ascertain. However, we took no chances and marched on, hugging the shelter of the walls on either side of the street.

In this formation we were met by the gaunt figure of old Joey—, our quarter-master. He fell in beside Major V—and guided us to our transport lines, a farm a little on the Ypres side of the town. Here we lay for half an hour munching biscuits and bully beef and watching an anti-aircraft gun shelling the aeroplane we had noticed before, which was now low enough to distinguish the sinister black crosses painted on its wings.

This was the reason for the extraordinary silence on the part of the guns, so skilfully hidden all around us.

The "Archibalds," as the anti-aircraft guns are popularly known, seemed to be making extraordinarily bad practice as the fleecy puffs of shrapnel burst all around the plane without apparent effect, and the machine, having spotted something, dropped a signal that burst into brilliant sparkles and turned for the enemy lines.

At this moment Joey returned from the outhouse concealing the telephonists with instructions that we were to proceed to the field, where the battalion was dug in at once.

CHAPTER 10

The Breaking In

We take the old road we have taken for years;
For you cannot cut corners in war, it appears.

The truth of this old maxim was impressed on us by the roundabout route we took to reach the field only a few hundred yards away where the remainder of the battalion lay.

Actually about two companies strong, they looked a mere handful as they lay huddled close to the hedges in the shallowest of shelter pits scratched in the soil with the field entrenching tool.

The draft was immediately ordered to "dig in," as the plane we had been watching a few minutes before had dropped its signal directly over this position.

We lost no time in digging more of these shallow pits, that reminded one rather gruesomely of graves, and had barely scraped them deep enough to roll into before a hail of small high-explosive shell fell all around us.

For half an hour the whoop and crash of falling and bursting shells kept us alternately ducking our heads and raising them again to see "where that one went," for curiosity is many times a stronger impulse than fear.

Curious things happened. A tree was cut in half by a shell, and the plumed top, falling clear of the stump, planted itself like a dart in the ground a few feet away.

A pack horse suddenly bolted across the open field with a slight cut on one flank, and half a dozen men made wild grasp at its bridle before one succeeded in recapturing the brute. And here and there groups of men finding their corner of the field a bit too "hot" for comfort would just as suddenly bolt across to another part and start feverishly digging in anew.

The shelling ended with as little warning as it had begun. There came a pause, and we thought naturally, "Well, thank God that's over!"—and said so. "Just a minute," said my companion; "there are the Three Sisters to come yet!"

Before one could say "Here they are!" the rush of much larger projectiles was heard, and in quick succession three heavy shells crashed into the foot of the field, throwing up black columns of smoke. "Those are coal-boxes," continued my tutor; "they used to have four guns in that battery, but they are only using three now."

The chuckle with which he added this last showed that he, at any rate, had no doubt as to the fate of the fourth gun.

This was evidently the end of the shelling, the enemy having, theoretically, made the field untenable. The actual casualties were, however, very slight, and the field entrenching tool, until now regarded as a toy, became a valued possession. We were already beginning to learn that the British infantry equipment is the finest in the world.

The shelling over, the draft was divided up amongst the remnants of the four companies, and Lyte and the writer had the good fortune to be placed with the same one.

Our company commander had been a lieutenant till a few days before, and was now a temporary captain. His senior subaltern was wearing a "British warm," the skirt of which had been riddled by machine-gun bullets, and a sergeant was to come out in orders that evening as an officer to take the remaining platoon.

A machine-gun duel in mid-air between one of our planes and an enemy machine that was eventually driven off and the dropping of some large shells into Ypres were the only other events of the day. Most of us slept, as there was work for us to do that night, until the joyful sound of "Tea up!" and the smell of hot "Maconachie" rations told us that supper was ready.

At 7 o'clock the battalion fell in to move up to the front line and dig some trenches. Hardly were we formed up when another violent shelling started, and we hurried back to the cover of our funk-holes.

Again the shelling was singularly ineffective, due, probably, to the fact that the enemy was using high explosive and not shrapnel. One shell by an unfortunate chance caught an artillery limber full of ammunition on the roadway, and it blew up with a sickening roar. The double report of this explosion evidently satisfied the German gunners, for a few minutes later the bombardment ceased and we again fell in.

The greatest secrecy was observed, and nobody but the guides knew our destination, and we followed them in silence up the shell-pitted road and across the pontoon bridge that spanned the Yser Canal. Various dark forms hobbled past, their baggy trousers showing them to be Algerians. A French outpost challenged us, and a party of Ghurkhas passed us leading pack horses with the bodies of their fallen officers lashed across the saddles. The Ghurkhas never leave an officer's body on the field, so the sergeant in rear of the platoon ahead informed us.

On either side of the road was a ruined trench, and even in the weird half-light of the flares we could see what a shambles they had become. The road was well called "Suicide Alley!"

Then suddenly we left the road and took to the open fields on the left, passing a trench occupied by some Imperial troops— it was our own first line trench. Then we knew what our work was to be; we were to dig an advance trench to link up with the French on our left and the English on our right. The advance continued up a gentle slope across which—nearly a thousand yards of bare bullet-swept field—the Ghurkhas had a day or so previously tried to charge. The bodies still lay there in rows just as they had fallen under the bursts of fire that mowed them down—pitiful huddled figures in the grass staring ahead into the great void. Few of the faces showed signs of suffering—such is the mercy of the rifle bullet; and so great was the resemblance to sleep that later, when we came to retire, the writer and others shook the bodies mistaking them for our own men.

In the midst of this ghastly scene, lit up by fitful glances of moonlight as clouds scudded over the sky, two companies moved forward, a long line of shadowy forms, to act as a covering party while the remaining half-battalion dug the new trench.

As we moved forward and lay down we could hear the thudding of the picks as they were driven into the ground, and from somewhere in the darkness ahead the *plick-plock* of the sniper began. Captain H——, our new company commander, passed down the line to warn us to count our men and see that all bayonets were fixed and magazines loaded.

The sniping increased, and a farmhouse ahead of us that had been smouldering for some time burst into flame. Two colts that were evidently confined near the blaze started to whinny and neigh, and a man who had been hit began to curse vilely.

From somewhere in rear a battery of French "seventy-fives" opened up with their ear-splitting reports, and we could see the outlines of the ruined farm ahead of us silhouetted against the crimson flashes of their bursting shrapnel. But of the enemy there was no sign—nothing but the arching trail of the flares that shot up and the steady *plick-plock* of the snipers. It was most trying.

It was nearly 2 o'clock before the trench was completed and we wakened our shivering men to retire, for so exhausted were they that, despite the cold and danger, many had dozed there on the body-strewn field with one hand firmly grasping the rifle. By this time traces of dawn began to show themselves in the eastern sky, and the moon seemed to flood the whole country with light.

Platoon by platoon in Indian file we drew off the field, carefully checking the count of our men as they passed until all were accounted for. Then the march back to billets began. And such a march! Worn out by the week's hard fighting, the older men staggered all over the road, all but dropping out from sheer exhaustion. Nor were the new men in better condition. Unaccustomed as yet to the weight of their packs, shaken by shell fire, and in some cases still weak from the sickness of the rough Channel passage, it was only sheer pride and the cruel taunts of the older men that kept them in the ranks. And thus we straggled on past the French outposts and over the Yser again, and on, on past the field we had lain in all day, on through Brielen to Vlamertinghe, back to billets. But the draft was broken in.

Chapter 11

Reserve Billets

It was only the prospect of several days of comparative rest that held us together at all as we floundered over the slippery cobble stones into Vlamertinghe. At the cross-roads that formed the battalion rendezvous in case of alarm, we got into some kind of military formation, for we spied the gaunt figure of the colonel there sitting his horse like a centaur. A grim man he was, who never spared his horses, himself or his men, and his only comment as we hobbled past was, "Dress up those fours!"—and tired as we were, the fours dressed up. When, however, Captain H—, who had gone to the rear of the company to chase up stragglers, came by, his greeting was a little more personal. "All well, H—?" he asked, and our gallant skipper answered, "All present, sir." It showed rather plainly the difference in feeling that existed for some time between those who had been through the Second Battle of Ypres and those who had not—a difference that it took much hard fighting to outweigh.

At last the company ahead turned down a side street, and we marched into our billet alone. It was a deserted warehouse with plenty of straw and quite comfortable, and, having got our men safely stowed away, the officers walked across the road to an empty house that formed our billets.

On the way H—pointed out the coffee wagon of which mention has been made. A sad-looking wreck it was, too, as a result of a stray shell. The ladies who had been in charge of it had been swooped down upon and gathered in by an irate provost-marshal some days before the shelling, and were, I am told, sent back to England for venturing so near the front line. The loss to the battalion was, however, immeasurable, as the ladies had been most devoted, and no matter at what hour the troops came in there was always a cup of coffee or soup awaiting them, and a smile—a smile that means so much to men whose hearts are lonely. Truly Raemaekers struck a key-note when, in his address in London, he asked England to "keep on smiling."

Arriving at the house, we found coffee ready and breakfast in the process of preparation. Bacon, an omelette, toast and marmalade (plum jam being out of season), it was a feast for the gods, any minor deficiencies being overcome by the keenness of our appetites. Then, having satisfied the inner man, we climbed the crooked little stairs to the bedrooms, where we found our bedding rolls stretched out on some mattresses the owners had left in their haste, and in three minutes we were asleep. Never did any bed seem more welcome.

We did not stay long in this billet, however, as we shifted the following day to a farm on the Brielen road. It was well we did so, for the enemy bombarded the town again and dropped one shell in our old billet a few hours after we left.

The farm we moved into is worthy of a little description, as it was typical of any farm in Flanders. The three buildings that constituted the house, barn, and cow byre were arranged in a hollow square around a brick courtyard, the centre of which was graced by a large pile of manure in an advanced stage of decomposition. Outside the square of buildings was a moat full of green slime and mosquito larvae. Here the men washed, and here, too, our buckets were filled each morning for the "lick and a promise" that served as a substitute for a bath.

Yet in spite of its unsanitary surroundings the house itself was beautifully clean inside, and no one could be healthier than the two buxom girls who formed part of the family that lived within. An exact census of the family was never obtained, as they poured out from nooks and crannies into the living-room occupied by us as sleeping quarters, generally at such awkward moments as when we were dressing or undressing. This was a matter of constant annoyance to Lyte, as the people persisted in

FIELD KITCHEN IN RESERVE BILLETS

announcing themselves with a *"Bon jour, monsieur,"* no matter what state of nudity they had caught you in.

We shared this room with an artillery officer, a young Irishman named Lee, who had a battery hidden somewhere near. We saw little of him, however, as we were generally falling in to move off when he came in for the evening, and when we returned after a night dug in in rear of some other troops, he was leaving to go up to his guns.

On some occasions we returned so late that the family were already up and at work, and instead of unrolling our valises we popped right into their beds. This was the subject of much joking of the simple peasant sort on the part of the young ladies, and consequent blushing on the part of poor Lyte. We all accused him of being their favourite, as he had nicknamed them "Ox-eye" and "Freckleface," names much more descriptive than the Marie and Jeanne their parents had chosen, and, having taken "Ox-eye" into our confidence, told her that poor Lyte was *"tres timide."* That was all she required, and from then on she directed all her charms toward him.

The next morning, his servant being as usual somewhere else, he ventured to ask for a little shaving water, in French of the first-steps variety. "Oh, *monsieur* speaks French," she answered, quite ignoring the mess-tin he held out. "Why did you not tell me?"—this last with an accusing glance at A—, the senior subaltern. Lyte began to deny all knowledge of the language, and she suddenly swung into English. "Nevair mind, I speak bloody good English," and then amidst our whoops of applause she demanded "It ees good? What!"

Lee came in one morning in a great state of excitement, his rich brogue being augmented with the news he brought. It seemed that on going up to his guns that morning he had found the farm there, till then occupied by a Belgian family, vacated and the white half-door—so familiar in all peasant countries where they keep pigs—placed lozenge-wise on the red roof. A hasty search revealed a partly burnt map and other papers of a military nature, and a German plane was already buzzing aloft. He had hurriedly withdrawn his guns; but siege guns take time to move, and before they could get away the shells were upon them and one gun crew had been practically wiped out. He was much excited, as became a man who had seen his first death.

We, too, had passed a very strenuous night. The Germans had commenced another attack on our line, using the gas again. We were wondering how much good the little respirators we were carrying would be, and the answer came soon enough.

As we moved forward we met men falling back gasping, coughing and sobbing, and the stink of their clothing was of hell's own reek, a choky mixture of chlorine and sulphur. "It's not war, mate; it's bloody murder!" was all one man gasped as he threw himself coughing on the ground, where he died before we moved on. It was not a pretty sight, and more than one rifle-butt was grasped the tighter and more than one oath sworn to get at the fiends who had let loose this vile poison, against which the only protection we had was a little pad of gauze to fasten over the mouth and nose after soaking in water from our water-bottles. These had been supplied by the thousand as soon as the authorities made known their wants by the women and children of England, and, feeble though this protection was, these simple little pads saved many lives that week.

But it was not our fate to meet the enemy again while in the salient. After continuing our march about another quarter-mile we lined a roadside and commenced digging another trench.

Here we lay and shivered all night, the men crouching in the trench, every fourth man alert and watching, the officers lying on the ground behind in shell holes or walking up and down swinging their arms and trying to keep warm. It was only one night of many.

The Germans continued to discharge gas against our line until May 15th, when they retook Hill 60. The bitter struggle of the past three weeks had begun as a mere counter-attack to our capture of this small but important mound.

By this time, however, the Canadians had been withdrawn, and we left the salient with few regrets. But somewhere on the German side of our trench line there are thousands of graves of our fellow-countrymen, and when the time comes for the balancing of accounts we shall expect these to weigh heavy in the scales.

Our brigade was the first to be relieved, marching out on the night of May 3rd, wondering vaguely where we were going, and also, perhaps, what would become of our friends "Ox-eye" and "Freckleface," with their stolid faces, their ample bosoms, and their square hips.

CHAPTER 12

Bailleul

Our next stop was Bailleul, a town of some fifteen thousand inhabitants just over the Franco-Belgian frontier. Possibly it was never known before the war, but it is now, for sooner or later everyone goes to Bailleul: it was, until the taking over of the line below Arras, the Mecca of the British Army.

But it was fifteen weary miles from Brielen, fifteen miles that we stumbled over in a drizzling rain on slippery cobblestones before turning up through an archway off the main street to our billets. Good billets they were, too—a loft with ample straw for one platoon, a school-house for the other three, and houses on another street for the officers.

In spite of the early hour, about 3 o'clock, Madame was up and around and soon made us fresh coffee and the inevitable omelette; then we clattered up the steep little stairs to bed. F—, the sergeant who had been promoted, joined us here and proved a jolly good sort. We went out to hunt up new billets the next day. He, being a Quebecker, acted as interpreter, as our room was too small and stuffy for two, and, moreover, looked into the operating-room of a hospital opposite.

We were fortunate in finding another billet quite close—an important point, as we were to mess together—and then took a stroll around the town.

Bailleul is, like most French provincial towns, arranged like a star, the Grande Place and Hotel de Ville forming the centre. We found our way to the cathedral, where a white-haired old *cure* showed us around, pointing out the door leading to the great square tower and the axe marks left by the German soldiers who burst it open. They had used the tower as an observing post during the week their cavalry had held the town the preceding October. The old man had been held as hostage by them, together with the mayor and some other notables, but when asked if he had been badly treated he was very non-committal. *"Qu'est-ce que vous voulez?"* he answered. *"C'est, la guerre!"*

That is the doctrine of humility taught France in 1870. *"C'est la guerre!"* It is used to explain anything from the shooting of civilians to the high cost of hand-made lace!

In a jeweller's on the Grande Place we obtained a little fuller information as to the Germans' actions. They had robbed Madame of all her rings, deliberately broken up all her watch glasses—there was not one to be obtained in the town—and smashed with their sword hilts the glass of her show-cases. And across the square they had confiscated all the champagne in a cafe, and when no more was forthcoming they piled the tables on the *pave* and burnt them; also she had heard—; but here F—'s patience had worn out, and as he said "Hearsay evidence is not admitted," so we said "Bonjour" and returned to billets.

Fortunately we did so, as we found we were slated to take a bathing parade at 1 o'clock and would barely have time to lunch. However, we caught the parade in time and marched the men to an old factory labelled "Divisional Baths." Here each man was supplied with a hot tub, soap and a clean towel, and was issued on stepping out from his tub with freshly-washed underwear, turning his soiled clothes in. This was a splendid system, and when later the clothes were not only washed but sterilised it ensured the men freedom for a short time at least from vermin.

It took some time running the whole company through in batches of forty, so we had a brief look around that part of the town. We also found that at the asylum officers could get a real bath—full length that one could stretch out in—at any time, but as it was late when our last man was ready to march off, we simply returned to billets.

We found the streets full of ambulances, most of them being

gas cases from around Hill 60, and, in spite of the respirators, most of them pretty bad cases.

Being somewhat of a chemist, I managed to see some of these cases a few days later. The hospital was so crowded that many cases were lying on stretchers in the garden that lies at the back of all these hideous perpendicular French houses, shielded from the weather by an awning only. But the worst cases were upstairs in a long hall—some eighteen of them, none of which had any hope. Reeking with chlorine, their faces a livid purple or an even ghastlier green, they lay there on the stretchers, each with a little bowl beside him, coughing his life away. And gradually the body would become weaker, the poor tortured lungs fail to clear themselves of the secretion that poured from their outraged tissue, and the fluid would accumulate slowly—oh, so slowly!—and the agonised victim died, not with the merciful swiftness of a bullet, but by gradual drowning.

This was the death that the Germans—ashamed of their own brutality—afterwards described as painless and merciful!

They may find justification for their crimes in Belgium, they may even smooth over the sinking of the *Lusitania*, but it must always be remembered that they, and they alone, are responsible for introducing into warfare this most ghastly and hideous death. It is said that German scientists spent years in perfecting this horror, practising its powers on plant life in the desert parts of Australia.

And the neutral nations—what of them? Are they not after all "accessories after the fact" and equally guilty? For, having sworn in solemn convention at the Hague to abstain from the use of asphyxiating gases, they entered no definite protest, though public opinion ran high on the subject.

Silence gives consent, and the poisoning of your enemy by chemical gases has now become the proper and chivalrous thing to do, and warfare has an added horror.

But the Allied chemists were at work devising means of lessening and preventing this danger, and already success was crowning their efforts; a new pattern respirator was devised and being issued, and a solution for dipping it in was already available. Dr. G——, of Queen's University, then serving as a subaltern in No. 2 Company, had been experimenting in private and devised a solution which varied only in the proportion of one of its elements from that adopted by the British Army, so we were probably the first brigade in the B.E.F. to receive this protection. Bottles of this fluid were carried by that long-suffering man the platoon sergeant, and parades held showing the men how to adjust and use the respirators.

Later we received flannel hoods, with mica windows, that had been dipped in the same solution, and these gave place in turn to the present gas helmet—a fearsome-looking affair, which, however, gives almost complete protection.

Our stay in Bailleul was enlivened by the arrival of a draft and the posting up of a schedule of training. The draft, needless to say, was the more welcome of the two. With the draft—who were magnificently-built men from the Middle West—we received a major who took command of the company, Captain H—dropping back as second in command. We thought this was rather hard lines, but H—made no complaint, though he felt it rather keenly, but finding our new man had the South African ribbon, we were a bit mollified.

Here, too, we held a memorial service for our fallen comrades, a powerful address being delivered by Major the Rev. William Beatty, one of the brigade chaplains. The troops, both old and new, were addressed, too, by Major-General Alderson, the divisional commander, who spoke of what the old men had done that the new men might understand what was expected of them, and stated that from now on he would count on us all as old troops.

Then we marched away feeling we were now a definite part of the old regiment, and a few days later started our trek southward.

We had entered another epoch!

CHAPTER 13

The Trek South

Until we left Bailleul the Canadian Division had been a part of the 2nd Army under Sir Herbert Plumer. We were now to go to the other end of the British line and become part of the 1st Army, then commanded by the present Commander-in-Chief, Sir Douglas Haig.

The news of this change was greeted with little enthusiasm by the old soldiers in our midst, but old soldiers are invariably pessimists, and imagine that every inspection is the prelude to more "dirty work at the cross-roads" and that every change made in their dispositions is for the worst.

Still, we were all sorry to leave Bailleul, with its bright little shops, and to say good-bye to the *cure* and our other friends there.

We fell in at night in the Grande Place—the little square that has probably seen more British troops come and go than any other town in northern France—and waited there for the battalion to form up. It was a beautiful summer night, the square tower of the cathedral and the Moorish spire of the Hotel de Ville forming perfect silhouettes against the starlit sky.

We were not kept waiting long; the shrill of a whistle from somewhere in the darkness put an end to all talking, and we hastily slung our packs on our shoulders again and started on our long tramp south to La Bassee.

For a while our route lay through country that some of us had traversed before, and Merville, Vieux Berquin, and other places were hailed with delight. There is a certain charm in returning to places that one has never expected to see again.

Much speculation began as to whether we were going back to our old trenches at Bois Grenier and Fleurbaix or not, but all hopes of this happening were dashed to pieces when, after passing through Neuf Berquin, we turned sharply to the right.

After this disappointment our packs began to weigh more heavily; the mouth organs and vocalists were less persistent in their efforts and gradually stopped in disgust, and only an accordion, wielded by a husky Scotchman at the rear of the company, strove to cheer us up. It was probably "Lochaber no more" or some other dirge he was playing, as he always showed unnatural fondness for the weird and the sad—probably due to the difficulty of fingering lively airs while on the march.

Passing through Merville, A—, who was marching beside me, regained his spirits sufficiently to point out a shop where a pretty girl sold champagne, and then relapsed into silence again.

A little further along the road we saw the adjutant riding alongside the major, and we knew we were nearing our billets. We turned up a side-road through Calonne, and the companies again broke off in different directions to the various farms to which they had been allotted.

We were again fortunate in getting very good accommodation—good airy barns, a mill-pond for washing, and a well of no-worse-than-the-ordinary water. But imagine our surprise to find chalked on the gate of the largest and best farm a sign:—

SMALL POX
BY ORDER

Here we were in a fix, as the men would not enter the place till we hunted up that long-suffering individual the interpreter. Then we found the placard to be only a ruse on the part of the unsophisticated peasantry to avoid having troops billeted there.

Having been found out and beaten at this game, Madame produced a sheet of paper she called a "reclamation," for some straw she claimed had been stolen by the preceding troops, and while she and the interpreter harangued over this we stowed our men away and sought our own billets a little distance up the lane.

At Calonne we received newspapers telling of the starting of the French offensive in the Artois district and prophesying an attack on our part to co-operate with them. We got out our maps and saw we were quite close to Neuve Chapelle, and as the Aubers Ridge—the great natural barrier to Lille—formed the obvious point to attack, we were not greatly surprised when a day or two after arriving at this peaceful little village we again took the route—this time toward Neuve Chapelle. We had heard the guns drumming along the Aubers Ridge all the day before during church parade service (May 9th), and were, on the whole, rather disappointed when after a few miles' march we turned off the road into a farm near *"le Cornet Malo"* and lay there in the mud all day. Some of the Lahore Division passed us on their way into the affair, the Indian gunners sitting on their limbers like statues.

It was rather a wretched day we spent in this farm. A heavy rain had turned the orchard in which we lay into a "bit of a bog," and all the straw we could buy or steal from the inhabitants could not keep us out of the mud. Here, too, we found the first instance of friction between the troops and the civilian populace, and the old lady made no bones about telling us how unwelcome we were. She opened hostilities by taking the rod from the pump so that we could not fill our water cart, and the troops retaliated by stealing bundles of unthreshed wheat. This was speedily put a stop to (and paid for) by the officers, and, for a while, peace reigned supreme while a thriving trade was done in coffee at two *sous* a cup and beer at three *sous* a glass.

Then some of the officers, seeing a lot of freshly-baked bread in a room just off the kitchen, offered to buy some. To our surprise the old woman started to wave a knife around dangerously and screamed: "You take my wheat, you take my water, and now you won't even leave me my bread! I would rather the Germans had come; they at least pay for what they take!"

As we had just paid her for the straw we thought this was going a little too far, and F—, who had a fine taste for sarcasm, waved his coffee-cup eloquently in the direction of the two slatternly girls that were peddling the coffee to the soldiers through

AMATEUR THEATRICALS BACK OF THE LINE

the window, and said "What? With all these beautiful daughters," and then continued with a graphic description of the horrors in Belgium.

This quieted the old lady down, but we were not sorry to leave there and shift to billets further up the road that night. It was the only instance we encountered of our being unwelcome in France, and the billet we occupied that night, although one of the filthiest houses we came across, was marked by a much more cordial spirit.

We were fortunate to get into this farm, as two of the companies had to bivouac, there being only accommodation for the staff and two companies in the area. The matter was decided by lottery, the major being lucky enough to draw a long straw.

It was rather a squeeze getting the company stowed away that night, but we managed somehow, and then turned into the kitchen. Here we were entertained with a graphic description by an old hag of how she had been wounded. It seemed that in some of the preliminary fighting she had run across a field between our troops and the Germans and received three bullets. She was quite cheerful about it and showed us two wounds, and when A— casually asked about the third she collapsed in a chair and went into spasms of laughter. All the rest of the evening she would point her finger at him and start again to tee-hee. A—was much annoyed.

We stayed in that vicinity another day, as it was not certain whether we would be thrown into support in the attacks on the Aubers Ridge at Fromelles or the Bois de Biez, but it was eventually decided that the artillery preparation had been inadequate, and the following night we continued our march southward.

Near Locon we passed some of the Indian Cavalry, gigantic-looking men with their turbaned heads. They surveyed us gravely as we passed, one or two flashing brilliant smiles in response to some friendly greeting. Then shortly afterwards we crossed the canal, and without further incident reached the outskirts of Bethune, where we went into bivouac in an open field, being favoured, most fortunately, with fine weather.

Our long trek had ended.

CHAPTER 14

Festubert, 1915

While the 4th Army Corps were trying to gain a footing on the northern end of the Aubers Ridge near Fromelles the 1st Army was making an equally desperate attempt to the south in front of Festubert, a village already in our hands.

But here, as at Neuve Chapelle, we found that the enemy front line, once penetrated, brought us in front of a series of strong points bristling with machine-guns, with dug-outs of almost incredible strength, some of them twenty and thirty feet under ground and safe against anything but the heaviest of field-guns, weapons that we were lamentably short of.

We could batter their front line to bits, for, like our own, it was situated on lower ground, and consisted of breastwork parapets owing to the water-soaked state of the whole plain; but their infantry would retire to these deep dug-outs, only emerging when their sentries warned them of the lifting of our fire to permit the attack.

We could, and did, drive the enemy from his front line, and once there we held on, but that was as far as we could go, for each of these strong points presented a new and entirely different problem to attack, and required a separate bombardment.

Our offensive had started on May 9th and reached its height about the 16th, by which time we had won ground to an average depth of six hundred yards on a front of four miles.

At daybreak on the 16th the 7th Division attacked in the direction of the Rue D'Ouvert and Canteleux, and by 7 o'clock had entrenched themselves in a line running roughly north and south, half-way between their original trenches and La Quinque Rue. The remainder of the day and the following night were spent in consolidating this position and trying to drive the enemy from some short trenches and posts that prevented this division from linking up with the 2nd Division on its left. This was accomplished by noon of the 17th, and by nightfall further ground had been gained to the right. Slight advances were also made on the 18th, but bad weather had greatly hindered the operation of our artillery.

On the 19th, the 2nd and 7th Divisions, having suffered very severely, were withdrawn, the latter being relieved by the Canadians.

Part of the 3rd Canadian Brigade had already become involved and had taken part in an attack on La Quinque Rue, where they succeeded in advancing the line some five hundred yards and linking up this ground with the Wiltshires on their right and the Coldstreams on their left.

Further advance was held up by one of the enemy's strong points known as the "Orchard." This position was naturally strengthened by a deep ditch full of water on three sides, besides hedges and wire entanglements.

During the afternoon of the 19th the Orchard was heavily bombarded by our guns, the shelling continuing till 7.45 p.m., when the Canadian Scottish advanced to the assault, supported by the 13th Royal Highlanders of Canada. Simultaneously the 48th Toronto Highlanders attacked some hundred yards to the right of the Orchard.

These attacks were made in broad daylight, and, despite the torrent of fire with which the enemy opposed them, the objectives were quickly gained, though the casualties were most severe, and by night the new line was consolidated.

Meanwhile the 2nd Brigade, which had been occupying trenches to the right of the Orchard, had attempted to take a position known as the "Bexhill Redoubt," but with less success, as the preliminary bombardment had been quite ineffectual.

Another bombardment of the position was made, and, supported by the Grenade Company of the 1st Brigade, a portion of the enemy's line to the right of the Bexhill Redoubt was gained and barricades erected and this portion held, in spite of a shelling that continued without ceasing the whole of the 22nd. The enemy attempted a counter-attack during the afternoon, but were repelled by our machine-gun and artillery fire. During the night the troops holding this line were relieved by Strathcona's and King Edward's Horse, then, of course, serving as infantry.

On the night of May 23rd the Bexhill Redoubt was taken by the 5th and 7th Battalions of the 2nd Brigade, reinforced by a squadron of the Strathcona's Horse. The captured positions were held all day, despite the enemy's bombardment—the heaviest shelling this brigade had yet experienced—and when they were relieved that night by the Royal Canadian Dragoons and the Eastern Ontario Battalion the brigade had lost 55 officers and 980 men.

The 1st Brigade, during these operations, had been occupying a portion of the line and suffering severely from shell fire. The writer's battalion, the Eastern Ontario, had relieved a battalion of the Black Watch on the night of the 19th near Indian Village. The Highlanders seemed glad to be leaving; one or two expressed their opinion that it was a "hell of a hole," a statement no one contradicted, as the place was vile with mud and stank from unburied corpses.

Between our line and the Western Ontario men, who held the old German trench ahead of us, lay hundreds of bodies that had been there since the last winter, for this narrow strip—not much more than a hundred yards in width—had been "No Man's Land." Attempts made by day and night to bury some of these bodies had to be given up, as the enemy swept the parapets of both trenches, on the least sign of movement, with "whizz-bangs." The Western Ontario Battalion suffered horribly, a constant stream of stretchers coming through our lines, starting with daybreak. These small shells were fired from light field-guns that had been brought up to the trenches, and were in consequence so close that the shell arrived and burst almost simultaneously with the report of the gun. Shells fired at the ordinary ranges announce their coming by a prolonged whirr, allowing a certain amount of time to get under cover before the burst comes.

We held this line till the night of the 24th, when we went forward to relieve the 3rd Brigade and consolidate the ground won by them. Each man carried two days' rations, a shovel, an extra bandolier of cartridges, and twelve sandbags, in addition to his ordinary fighting equipment.

Most of the companies had some kind of trench to start work on, but at our end there was nothing but a line marked out by the engineers. Listening posts and covering parties were sent out, and by morning we were occupying a ditch about three feet deep with a fairly good parapet in front. No fires were permitted, as we were hidden by grass from the enemy and the trench was not yet in shape to stand any bombardment.

The next night we were fortunate in obtaining more sandbags and some timber from a German trench we had passed on the way up. Some mail and parcels of food came up, and we managed to clear out our wounded. Most welcome was ammunition for the flare pistols the officers carried. We had come into the trench with six rounds for each pistol and had been carefully saving them in case the enemy attacked.

Our parapet was now high enough to be easily visible to the enemy, and we received considerable attention from his snipers and artillery the following day. No serious damage was done, however, and we were relieved the following night by a Territorial battalion of Highlanders.

On the 26th General French, having attained for the moment the immediate object in view, ordered a curtailment of the bombardment and a consolidation of all positions won, and the Battle of Festubert came to an end.

By the 31st of the month the whole Canadian Division had been withdrawn and lay in reserve billets around the outskirts of Bethune.

CHAPTER 15

Carpe Diem

"Home again!" said Begbie Lyte as he watched his servant unrolling his valise in the little field we had left a fortnight before, and the rest of us laughed, for he voiced the thoughts of all.

It required a bit of an optimist to see a home in that apparently comfortless situation, but men just relieved from the firing line are not over-critical, and the prospect of a night under the stars, but away from the crash of shell and the *"phit"* of striking bullets, was pleasant enough to satisfy the most chronic grouser.

We had, of course, only reached this billet about dawn, so without wasting any time over such niceties as washing we bundled our clothes into a sort of pillow in the head of our "Wolseleys" and drew from the depths of that wondrous combination of a valise and bed that luxury of luxuries on active service, a pair of pyjamas, and were soon dozing comfortably in dreamland.

Our men, lacking such comforts as Wolseley valises and pyjamas, merely denuded themselves of their equipment, and, with perhaps a preliminary search for "trench pets," slept in their greatcoats under shelters rigged up with waterproof sheets. They had no blankets, for it was summer, and blankets and rum issue are alike "Nah pooh" on the 1st of June. We had in fact turned in our blankets before starting southward from Bailleul.

Here and there bivouac fires had been lighted, and round them small groups sat and talked over our recent losses. In another day they would mention them no more, though they would never forget them.

Presently even these fell asleep, and when, a few hours later, the moon showed herself between the clouds she looked down on a still and silent camp, the only signs of life being the dying embers of the fires and the dark forms of the sentries moving slowly up and down the field.

Custom permitted us to sleep on till noon the next day, and then everybody had a grand clean up. A shower-bath was extemporised by the simple process of standing over a ditch naked and unashamed while a patient batman, with the aid of what is called, in official language, "one pail, collapsible canvas," poured water over until, breathless but refreshed, the victim shouted to stop. Later on sundry private soldiers whom one had known in civil life would approach and ask for the loan of the pail. Such is democracy in the "Colonials."

Bath being over, the razor was vigorously applied and a week's growth scraped painfully from sunburnt chins, on which talcum powder was afterwards daubed in copious quantities till we smelt to heaven like a Gaiety chorus!

Then breakfast! Its fragrance had been tantalising our noses during all this gay preliminary, for dirty as we may get—and yet sit down to eat in the trenches—it was an unwritten law that no man who was not shaved, shorn, and washed after the manner of the Romans should sit down to mess when in reserve. Lyte one day in a burst of enthusiasm, while treasurer of the mess, decreed that the servants should also wash before starting to cook, but after one trial, dinner being thereby delayed a couple of hours, the mess rebelled and the cooks were allowed to revert to their former state of barbarism.

Breakfast over, there came the censoring of mail, so that it could be sent to battalion headquarters before 2 o'clock. This is supposed by some to furnish an endless amount of amusement to the officers, and often facetious remarks are introduced by the writer to this end, but to most of us censoring is a beastly bore, and one views with dismay the enormous pile of letters that your platoon sergeant dumps down on your bed each day at noon with the laconic announcement of "Mail, sir!"

One runs across people of many sorts while reading through this heap. The first and commonest is the married man who sticks strictly to private affairs and perhaps says to his wife: "You remember Jimmy D— who used to work at So-and-so's. He was killed by a shell, but you can tell his wife he didn't suffer none, as he died quick." Not a word you will notice of his own escape or of anything that would tend to aggravate the sorrow of the stricken family. Of the same affair he would probably write to a chum: "You know poor old Jimmy D—. He was all blew to hell by a whizz-bang. A chunk of it just missed my napper by an inch. I come near going West that time, believe me!"

Then there is another type whose endless exaggerations make one wish to scribble the word "liar" at the end of each paragraph, but which you pass, after scratching out the numbers of our slain and some of the grosser statements.

Once in a while you may come across a guileless sort of man who, after extolling the virtues of his platoon commander, proceeds to tell his friend Bob: "No, I haven't been made a corporal yet, but our section has none now and I am the oldest soldier left." One feels great curiosity as to the state of this paragon's conduct sheet.

However, these are mere details. The great joy of being in reserve billets is the ability to go, after parades, of course, into the nearest town and spend the 125 francs that the paymaster exchanges once a month for a Bank of Montreal cheque. The private soldier, receiving a meagre 30 francs a month, has to content himself with simpler joys than champagne (vintage 1914) and hand-made lace. Instead he partakes of French beer at three *sous* a glass, and his friends overseas receive hand-embroidered postcards of brilliant but patriotic designs worked by the crippled children of Paris.

The greater part of the soldiers' money, however, is spent on food—dainties such as oatmeal, sardines, canned fruit, and so forth—and little shops close to the firing line welcome the twice-monthly visit of the paymaster.

Bethune, the town outside of which we were at this time billeted, was quite the gayest place we had visited since leaving Poperinghe.

"Business as usual" was its motto, in spite of the almost daily shelling it received by light guns, said to have been mounted on an armoured train.

This bombardment took place, as a rule, between 6 and 7 o'clock each evening, but the damage done was very slight, only one soldier being reported killed during our stay. There were civilians killed at various times, but from a military point of view the shelling was absolutely useless.

If, perchance, one was taking tea with Marie, or anyone else for that matter, and the shelling started, it was quite the thing to seek the shelter of the cellar and stay there *"en famille"* until the bombardment was over, when you would emerge, Mademoiselle perhaps pushing a loosened hairpin back in place, and continue to enjoy your tea.

It was not everyone's fortune to have this happen, however.

The bank took a more serious view of the affair, and, having sandbagged the cellar windows, posted notices stating that, in the event of shelling, customers could continue business in the cellar. And this was in a nation that we have always looked upon as effeminate and excitable!

Under these pleasant circumstances, plus a little setting-up drill and "physical jerks," we passed a very pleasant fortnight before going into the trenches again—this time at Givenchy.

CHAPTER 16

Givenchy, 1915

It was now the turn of the 1st Brigade to emulate the gallant deeds of the 2nd and 3rd Brigades at Ypres and Festubert, and right gallantly they did so.

Givenchy, while receiving but slight mention in Sir John French's dispatches, was perhaps only a minor affair; but the fact that, owing largely to a shortage of bombs, we were unable to hold the ground we had gained does not in any way detract from the gallantry of the attack. Comparisons with Hulluch or Loos cannot be made, as we had nothing like the support of either infantry or guns that were available on those later occasions.

The Canadians relieved the Guards in the Givenchy trenches during the second week in June. Our brigade was still in reserve around Bethune when they passed us; the Prince of Wales, a slim, tired-looking boy in khaki, marched by with his regiment. It wasn't often we had any of the Royal Family march past us; generally the boot was on the other leg!

We entered the trenches at night and, as usual, in a drizzling rain. Except for the fact that it was miserable weather, that we had followed the La Bassee Canal in, and that he had a jumping toothache, the writer has no vivid impressions of that night.

We lay in some trenches just in front of the ruined distillery, dug in a commanding mound that had been thrown up in building the canal, and stayed there till next night, when we moved forward again, two companies going into the front line and two, one of them the writer's, occupying a support trench.

Here we learned what work was, every bit of food, bombs,

The distillery at Givenchy

and ammunition required for the front line being carried up these narrow twisted communication trenches by the support companies, for the proximity of our line to the enemy would not permit of taking a single man from the front line. It was the one time we cursed the heavy mailbags that arrived with unceasing regularity every night.

The right of our trenches here rested on the canal, and could go no further forward owing to a small marsh that lay in front. But about the centre of the position the line swooped forward into a small and dangerous salient known as the "Duck's Bill."

It was opposite here we proposed to attack, the actual objective being the high ground between points H2 and H3 on the map. If we and the 7th Division on our left could gain this high ground it would straighten out this dangerous salient and give us a footing on the Aubers Ridge.

Great preparation was made for this attack. A mine that had been under construction for months was to be sprung, and we were to give the Hun a bombardment such as he had never had before.

Two field-guns were brought up on the night of the 14th and placed in epaulements that had been dug in rear of the front-line trench to receive them. They were to be kept masked till the last moment before the attack, when they would cut wire and silence machine-guns along the front over which we were to attack.

The Central Ontario Battalion was to make the attack, supported by the Toronto Battalion, while the Eastern and Western Battalions were to man the captured trench, consolidate it, and provide for any counter-attacks. On the left, the East Yorks and another battalion of that brigade were to co-operate.

Meanwhile the mine was being hastily completed, and by noon on the 15th it was ready for firing, the explosive being carried up by Lyte and his satellites from near the distillery. They had had rather a bad time of it crossing the Pont Fixe, a wrecked bridge that was under observation from the German position.

The Huns, seeing the first load of these white boxes being carried over the bridge, laid a gun on it and when the second

Our support trenches at Givenchy

party came across opened fire on them, wounding several men close to F—, the Quebecker, who as junior sub. was bringing up the rear. He, however, kept the men from dropping the explosive, and the party reached the mine shaft without any further casualties.

Our three days' bombardment, which had started on the night of the 13th, now died down slightly, and the Germans, having had ample time to bring up their reinforcements, waited for the attack.

At 3 o'clock our two companies in the front line drew off to the right and the men of the Central Ontarios took their places, while the communication trenches leading up were choked with the Toronto men who were to form their supports. Our artillery now tuned up again and caught the Germans by surprise. They, in turn, shelled us heavily, causing many casualties owing to the crowding of the trench.

A— and the scout-corporal went up the trench and were caught by a shell and the corporal was killed, A— being fortunate in escaping, though very severely wounded.

Another shell lit fairly on a bomb depot about this time and destroyed one of our reserves of these weapons, and a third shell killed Lieutenant-Colonel Beecher, the second in command of the attacking battalion.

The two guns in the front line had been unmasked and were cutting wire with desperate rapidity, though their crews were practically wiped out a few moments later, and in the midst of this turmoil the mine went up.

It was quite the largest mine that had been exploded along the front, and the tremor of the earth could only be compared to an earthquake.

So eager was the engineer officer to reach the German trench, that, finding he was striking water underground, he loaded in something like a ton and a half of explosive to make certain. Thus he achieved the double result of winning the Military Cross for his skill and blowing up a portion of our front line, from which fortunately our men had been withdrawn.

But a number of our own men were killed and wounded,

AFTER GIVENCHY
Left to right: Capt. Birdsall, Winnipeg Brown, Ponton, Capt. Richardson, Gutty

and, what was far worse, another reserve depot of bombs was buried under the debris of the explosion.

In the meantime, masked by the fountain of earth thrown up by the mine, the attack had been launched and was already in the first German line, the bombers were beginning to work along the trench to the right and left, and the little flags that marked their progress could be seen moving slowly to the left to link up with the East Yorks.

But the East Yorks had been unable to advance owing to the wire not having all been cut and the machine-gun fire that enfiladed them from their flanks.

Meanwhile the Canadians had gained the third German line, but already the shortage of bombs was beginning to be felt, and they were forced back to the second line, where they established blocks in the trench and were able to hang on until the following day, when the German counter-attack forced them to fall back to our own front line.

The brigade had lost heavily. Of twenty-three officers of the Central Ontario Battalion who went over the parapet only three returned uninjured, the remainder being either killed, wounded, or missing!

Nor had the Yorks fared much better.

During the second day of the affair the writer was moving up a narrow communication trench with a platoon carrying ammunition to the front line when he encountered a party of about the same strength coming down the trench in defiance of a notice board marked "In only." After asking in vain for the officer in charge of the party he was told "For God's sake, sir, we aren't any party. We're all that's left of two companies!" There was nothing left to be said!

Once again it had been proved that attacks by daylight, unless supported by masses of supports, are bound to fail.

The 2nd Canadian Brigade relieved us, marching in by one side of the canal while we marched out along the other. We called across our best wishes to them as we passed. We had, it is true, been heavily pounded, but we were far from being depressed, though we might well have been.

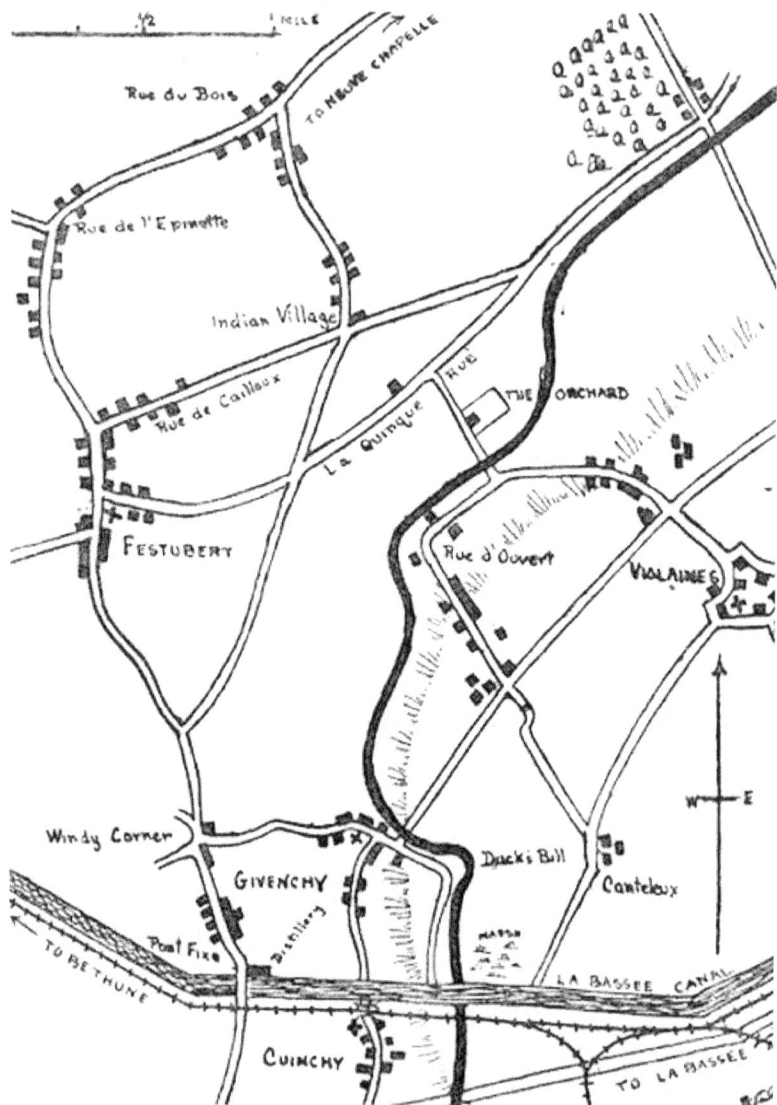

APPROXIMATE LINE AFTER FESTUBERT AND GIVENCHY, 1915

Instead, as we passed an electric towing machine lying neglected along the towpath, a man in the ranks behind asked his mate what they were used for.

"Don't you know?" was the reply as he glanced at the broad-tyred wheels; "why, they use them for rolling down the water in the canal after a storm!"

It was in this mood we returned to billets.

CHAPTER 17

Northward Again

After Givenchy the Canadian Division rested for another week around the outskirts of Bethune before starting its long tramp back to the northern end of the line again.

But it was far from being a week of idleness, and hard drilling was the order of the day. Great stress was laid on bomb-throwing, and, in spite of the heavy casualties the bombing sections had suffered, there was no dearth of volunteers for the "Suicide Club," as the bombers termed themselves. The men, as well as the officers, recognised the value of this weapon, old as the use of gunpowder itself, but now reinstated to greater importance than ever before.

So we started northward, a very uneventful and tiring march, our first stop being at Neuf Berquin, where we rested a day.

The march had been very fatiguing; it was the latter end of June, and "sunny France" had been living up to her reputation, and even the nights, in which we marched for the sake of coolness and concealment, were most oppressive. And it was in weather like that that the famous "First Seven Divisions" fought and marched twenty-five or thirty miles, dug in and fought again, only to have again to retire!

And we were only averaging fifteen miles a march! Our next halt was at Noote-Broome, a mere hamlet, where we held church service and then marched straight into the trenches.

This was a new area for us. We had grown so accustomed to shifting from one part of the line to another that we had already nicknamed ourselves the "Canadian Foot Cavalry."

However, we were fated to rest in that vicinity for several months, though our brigade shifted from one position to another along that line all summer.

We first relieved a battalion of the Middlesex on June 28th opposite a poisonous little spot known as *"la Petite Douve."* Here a small stream, dignified by the name of the Douve River, wandered lazily across the flat at the foot of the Messines Ridge and coiled like a natural moat in front of the Petite Douve Farm.

This, like all farms in Flanders, was a square of strongly-built brick buildings. In it the enemy had established concrete machine-gun positions and converted the place into a veritable fort. It projected in a salient from their average line and enfiladed the main road running from our position to Messines.

The Middlesex, on our relieving them, had told us a weird tale of the number of rounds of rifle ammunition they expended in a single night. We discounted this by the usual 50 per cent., but our major had an extra supply brought up in case of emergencies.

An evening or two later we found the reason for the Middlesex's heavy expenditure of cartridges, for the enemy, on a three-mile front, suddenly opened up rapid fire, keeping up this fusillade for nearly half an hour.

This occurred at odd intervals for some time while we occupied that front, and was known as "the Germans (or the Fritzes) getting their wind up." The Middlesex had been trying to beat down this fire with their own rifle fire; we contented ourselves with sitting tight and, by careful patrolling, watching for the first signs of an attack. On such a night as this poor F— was out on patrol when the rapid fire opened up, and we nearly struck him off the company strength. Much to our surprise he and his patrol came in later, quite unhurt, having discovered, and taken shelter in, an advanced German trench near some willows.

Later it became quite the thing to take a few men out with you and bomb this trench.

We only did two "tours" in this particular piece of trench, as the next time we came in that company frontage had been allotted to the battalion on our left and we moved just around the corner, the Petite Douve Farm being almost hidden from our view by trees but continuing to annoy us with its machine-guns.

It was here that we celebrated "Dominion Day" (July 1st), a Canadian ensign that had arrived a few days before in a parcel from "home" waving gaily behind our lines.

It was here, too, that Captain Frank Tidy, of the Toronto Battalion, astonished the brigade by making a sortie from the trench in daytime and bringing in two prisoners whom he had observed moving in the tall wheat that here and there shut off our view of the German line.

Much courage is required to make a sortie of this sort, and one is not surprised that a third German had to be shot before the other two surrendered to Captain Tidy and his two comrades.

No information of importance was gained from these prisoners except that the enemy had sent them out to ascertain who the new troops occupying our line were.

Summer was now well advanced, and it was doubtful if a further "push" would be attempted that season, and we gradually settled down to the routine of trench warfare.

During the middle of July we did one tour in the trenches in front of Wulverghem, relieving a battalion of Northumberland Fusiliers. We only stayed there a few days, but were greatly bothered with rifle-grenades, so, finding that our grenades fell short of the German line, the major and a small party took the grenade-gun out in the long grass until they were able to reach the enemy and thus secured a temporary peace.

The East Yorks then relieved us, and when next we entered the trenches it was a little to the right of our old position and in front of the celebrated Ploegsteert Wood.

Here the right battalions of the brigade had rather a strenuous time, as some mines had been exploded and there was still a struggle going on around the craters.

But on the left, abutting our old position near the Douve Farm, we had rather an easy time of it, there being little shelling and the trenches nearly two hundred yards apart.

In fact our greatest activity was at night and at dawn, condi-

Entrance to Plugstreet Wood

tions at the latter time being well expressed in an anonymous sonnet we found pinned up in a dug-out entitled *Stand To*:

Early every morning,
As the stars begin to tire,
Without the slightest warning,
Our maxim opens fire;
A German gunner answers back,
And one by one the rifles crack,
All down the line you can hear the rattle,
And then begins our morning battle;
And as the dawn creeps in the sky
A couple of shells go whistling by.
The bullets are flying in every direction
Just as the larks begin to carol,
And all because the machine-gun section
Wanted to warm their hands on the barrel.

CHAPTER 18

Nights of Gladness!

Our nights around Ploegsteert fully made up for the peacefulness of the days, and "No Man's Land" between the two lines of trenches became the scene of many exciting adventures. This was particularly true of the area directly in front of us, as a large bean field extended from the German line nearly to ours. It was a dull night indeed that our listening post did not either bomb, or get bombed by, an enemy patrol. Casualties, though, were fewer than one would expect from such combats, as bombs are very local in their action, and it was not easy to locate the enemy's position exactly by ear as he rustled his way through the beans.

Behind the lines there was less romantic work; for General Joffre, in an odd moment, had sent a circular letter to the various divisions calling attention to a new form of trench for protection against shell fire, and we dug these trenches till there was hardly a foot of Allied soil unturned. Later, during the rains, we drained our living trench into them on the principle that the uncomfortable sensation experienced during a heavy shelling would act as a distraction to the inconvenience of standing in several feet of water.

While we were in these trenches the enemy fired the dry yellow grass in "No Man's Land" a few nights after their capture of our line at Sanctuary Wood, near Hooge, with the flame projectors or *flammenwerfers*. A hurried "stand-to" was ordered, as we thought a similar attack was about to be made.

But the fire died down and we saw no signs of the enemy

coming over. It was, however, an anxious night, and great interest was taken in widening our wire entanglements as more and more details of the Hooge affair trickled down to us. How we longed for a supply of the iron stakers that our patrols brought in time after time from the German wire! We got them, too—later.

Later the Germans could not have burned down our wire, even had they tried, as a week of heavy rains came on, and, on such trifles do the fates of nations hang, these had a most serious effect on the "Autumn Push"—it was already September—as our offensive around Hulluch and Loos was called.

We were in reserve during the first two days of the attack, and received with clock-like regularity the *communiques* telling of our successful advances.

Our gunners were co-operating by the process known as "engaging the enemy's artillery," but we did not doubt that the Toronto Battalion, then occupying our trenches, were having rather a warm time of it, as the Hun, instead of being a sportsman and shelling our batteries, used to retaliate on our trenches.

We set off the following day for the trenches. It had started to rain about 4 o'clock, so that by 7, when we reached the head of Mud Lane, we had no reason to doubt the origin of this homely name.

In pleasing contrast to our growlings and grumblings as we took their places, the Toronto men filed out prophesying all sorts of cheerful things in store for us. All we could see ahead of us was plenty of work, for the shelling they had received had smashed down our bulwarks and annihilated the officers' kitchen—rather an elaborate structure, of which we were justly fond—and they, in the sure and certain knowledge of a relief, had only cleared away enough of the debris to make the trench passable.

Meanwhile our listening posts, soothed with a wee drappie o' rum, went over the parapet laden down with waterproof sheets fully determined to make the best of a bad job, our sentries were posted, and the welcome order to "Stand down" came along the trench. Those of us not otherwise occupied turned into our dug-outs and were soon asleep. After a certain stage one becomes unconscious to even a revolver-butt prodding one in the ribs.

Our trenches, Plugstreet Wood

It seemed only a few minutes before the sergeant thrust his head into my dug-out with a "Midnight, sir!" I groped around for my pocket lamp and looked at my watch—some way you always hope the sergeant is wrong, but he never is—and tumbled out to relieve poor Lyte, who had spent a miserable four hours.

A rift in the clouds showed our friends of the midnight watch—the Great Bear and Cassiopeia—twinkling merrily as though it had never rained for a fortnight.

I sloshed my way down to the far end of the trench. Pools of water lay ankle deep here and there along its length. Already one or two men, who had just come off sentry, had started to drain these into little catch-pools. From here it was baled by means of the ever-useful Maconachie tin into an equally useful biscuit tin, which was afterwards dumped on the enemy's side of the parapet.

In other places the men had turned in and were already asleep, so they were promptly stirred up and told to "Get busy," and, for the night, the *blosh* of the baling tin took the place of the smack of a shovel on a freshly-placed sandbag.

At frequent intervals it was necessary to crawl out and visit the listening posts, who lay in the rank grass just beyond our own wire.

On returning, not only were one's feet wet, but knees and elbows as well. Then it was up and down the trench again for another hour or so.

A fine drizzle set in and the stars again disappeared, the drizzle turning to a steady shower.

I retired to company headquarters, only emerging when necessary to visit the sentries and listening posts again. There, by the aid of a sputtering candle, I sought diversion in the shape of a sevenpenny novel that some kindly soul had forgotten in his haste to be relieved.

Just as I reached the stage where I could sort the various characters into their ultimate roles of hero, villain, and heroine the sergeant again intruded with the news that one of the listening posts reported an enemy patrol approaching. A few flares were fired up, but revealed nothing except a white glare of grass

Our trenches at Plugstreet

field, the bean patch, and the inky black of a few willows with our listening posts huddled at their bases. These men were, of course, invisible to the enemy, as the flare had fallen between their line and the willows. A flare must fall behind the object aimed at to reveal anything with accuracy.

Even a couple of parachute lights fired from "Little Archibald," as we called the special gun used for these larger flares, revealed nothing, so I gave up in disgust, woke the only two men who had not been disturbed all night, tied a couple of sandbags around each knee, and once again disappeared over the parapet.

An hour later, on returning, the signaller warned me it was time for the "situation" report. I scrawled out the usual formula, "Situation unchanged; enemy quiet; wind northerly," and handed him the form.

It was ten minutes late, and though the adjutant would not read it till morning I knew I was in for a wigging. Wet and disgusted I turned to my dug-out.

A few minutes later traces of dawn showed themselves in the east. The rain ceased and a fine mist took its place. The men stumbled out to their rifles in response to the order "Stand to," and I made a final promenade of the trench, dragging out a man here and there who was tardy.

Then I stirred up the officer of the day and handed over my duties. The mist cleared away, showing the German line, grim and formidable as ever! Another day had dawned.

It was on such a dawn as this that poor Jack L—, my platoon-sergeant, was killed. The fog had lifted a little, revealing an enemy patrol to our listening post.

He, taking the nearest two men with him, went out in search of them, and a flare falling near the little party showed them up to the enemy snipers. He alone was hit. We buried him in the battalion cemetery the next day, the colonel reading the service over his body, and we thought as we lowered him into his grave what a very good friend he had been.

It was not very many days later that we changed from this brigade area to another, leaving Ploegsteert with its memories, sad and otherwise, behind us.

CHAPTER 19

In Front of Messines

The Second Canadian Division arrived in France during our stay in Ploegsteert, and after a short rest took over a sector on the right of St. Eloi and in front of Messines.

Here it was that we relieved them about a fortnight later—our third move while in front of this grim hill, the scene of such hard fighting in October of the year before.

The line at this point swung forward in a small salient to within fifty yards of the enemy—the only footing we now held on this famous ridge—and to the Toronto and Eastern Ontario Battalions fell the honour of guarding this point all winter.

Here, too, we were to learn something of grenade and mine warfare such as the other two battalions of our brigade had been waging all summer near Ploegsteert.

And the little graveyard in rear of the line was to receive the bodies of many of our comrades and hold them in common sanctity with those of other gallant men, British and French, Highlanders and Turcos, who had perished on the slopes of Messines.

For a week we systematically registered our guns on new points in the enemy's second and third lines—the usual preliminary to an offensive—and bombarded them severely.

This was done to prevent the enemy from moving any of his guns from this area to the southern end of the line, where, now that the weather was again favourable, the British were to make another thrust.

For this purpose, too, we were to make a "little demonstration" on our front, using smoke bombs to make the enemy believe we were going to use gas, and, to our great satisfaction, it was announced that in those areas where the real offensive was being made the Germans would be treated to a dose of their own poison. Too long we had waited and allowed the enemy to use this fearful weapon against us, thinking the neutral nations might intervene; but their interest in the cause of humanity was largely a financial one, and we determined to adopt a broader view, perhaps, of what justifiable weapons are, and make use of the advances of science. France was already using the gas, but Britain hesitated at setting her hall-mark on such a usage, necessary as it had become.

The day, October 13th, was ideal for observation, beautifully clear, with a gentle breeze from our trench towards the enemy's. Nothing finer could be desired for our operations to the south.

About 2 o'clock our guns, along the whole British front, started to cut wire as though preparing for an attack.

The Germans in return sprinkled our lines vigorously with shrapnel, the fleecy white puffs of their shells showing up like clouds on the clear blue sky.

From our trench on the hill top we could see the long line of trenches, hidden here and there by trees, stretching southwards to Armentieres, the tall chimneys of which were clearly discernible.

Anxiously we glanced from this view to our watches while the hands crept slowly around to the appointed moment. In the distance there suddenly appeared faint lines of whitish smoke among the trees; and we lit our smoke bombs and hurled them over the parapet. There was a moment's pause, and then they burst into clouds of yellow smoke, hiding the German trench from view.

The tone of their bombardment changed immediately, and crashing salvoes of high explosive fell around us.

Our guns paused for a moment, and the crisp rattle of musketry, the droning of myriads of bees, and the bursts of machine-gun fire were heard alone as they ran through whole belts of cartridges; then all minor sounds were again drowned out by the clashes of our shells as they burst all along the German front line.

THE START OF THE SMOKE CLOUDS
The Little Demonstration, October 13th, 1915

Gradually the smoke cleared away as the bombs burnt themselves out and showed that no attack was being attempted. The bombardment slackened, though the Germans continued to shell us heavily till almost dusk, but with little further effect except that they rendered the evacuation of our wounded more dangerous.

Our casualties had, however, been slight, but it was simply marvellous luck, for our parapets were ruined heaps and the trenches filled with debris.

We gazed sadly around, knowing it meant many nights of hard work to restore these, and mentally decided to join the artillery in the next war, as they alone had enjoyed the afternoon's work.

The German guns had certainly been kept busy, and it was some consolation to read in their report of the affair that "an attack using gas on a thirty-mile front had been repulsed with heavy losses to the enemy."

We had produced the desired effect.

Below La Bassee the 46th Division had been equally successful and gained the Hohenzollern Redoubt, while on their right in the vicinity of Loos the 4th Corps were holding nearly twelve hundred yards of German front-line trench.

It had been a good day's work, but summer was now over and good weather could not be depended on, so no further offensive was made, though fighting of the most stubborn and desperate sort took place around the newly-gained ground, which was, however, successfully consolidated.

During the remainder of the month, except for the exploding of a mine and aerial activity, there was little that occurred on the Canadian front.

CHAPTER 20

Mine Warfare

Among the other things we took over from the outgoing battalion when we first moved into this position was the care and continuance of a mine, and this mine was to form our chief worry as long as we held that line.

At first we were inclined to regard the mining officers—of which we had two—as a sort of nuisance like engineers, trench mortar men, and some others, who were always demanding men for carrying and working parties. But we were not long in finding that they were, like ourselves, necessary evils, and they became welcome guests at our little mess when in the trench.

Whenever the trenches approach as close as they did at this point mine warfare becomes inevitable, and it is a game at which it is best to be first.

To defend a position against this method of attack one commences a counter-mine at a depth sufficient to take the gallery or tunnel underneath the enemy's one, which, once it is located, is blown in before they manage to get under the defenders' trench. The tunnel or gallery is barely large enough for a man to crawl along on his hands and knees, and must be boarded foot by foot as it progresses to prevent it from collapsing.

In this cramped position the sapper wields his pick, a peculiar affair not unlike a harpoon, and scrapes the loosened earth back with a short grubber to another man who removes the earth in sandbags.

Progress under such circumstances must be slow, but it is made slower by the necessity of running galleries at right angles to the main tunnel from time to time in an effort to locate the enemy.

Here men are posted, while all work is for a time stopped, to listen for the first sounds of the enemy's sappers—the thud-thud of the picks or the "cough" of the man whose lungs seek this relief in the stuffy air of the cramped tunnel.

If the enemy is not found, progress is continued forward from both ends of the cross-gallery and the game goes merrily on.

About this stage the mining officer will, if you happen to be holding the trench under which he is grovelling, wax eloquent over a crumpled sheet of tracing linen that he presents to your view as a diagram of the workings. It looks like nothing so much as a drawing of the kith and kin of an old and prolific family; but you dare not tell him that, or he will be your enemy for life.

Instead you should say, "Ahem!" and "Oh, yes; how clever!"—then he will ask you for only ten instead of twelve men on the night's working party.

But once the enemy is located you begin to regard him more seriously, for on his skill depends the life of every man in the trench above, and a false change in direction may mean missing the enemy's tunnel altogether.

Sometimes, but not often, the mining is so quietly done that the first sign of the enemy is the sudden collapse of the wall of earth between the two galleries, leaving the rival workers face to face!

At other times, and this is a normal occurrence, the enemy are heard to one side or the other, and a small charge of powder is laid and his gallery is blown in, crushing his workers to death, or perhaps merely burying them to perish miserably by suffocation.

To prevent this occurring men are kept in the ends of all the passages listening for the tap-tap of the picks that spells danger!

If the picks are heard for a while and then stop, there are anxious moments, for it may mean that the enemy has located our workers and decided to blow first and wreck our galleries, or it may mean the explosive is already in place and ready for firing, or perhaps only a change in the direction of the enemy's tunnel.

The situation is not a pleasant one for either the men in the trench above or the sappers in the galleries below, and on the mining officer's decision much depends.

It was while we were breakfasting one morning that the corporal in charge of the underground sentries reported that the enemy could be heard working in No.— gallery.

This was the third time since taking over the mine that tapping had been reported, and both the preceding times had proved to be the result of overstrained imaginations. Captain H—, our skipper, had on both occasions descended to the bowels of the earth and listened patiently for half an hour, emerging again disgusted with things in general.

This time he motioned to the writer to accompany the corporal, and together we made our way to the mine, shedding our jackets and belts at the head of the shaft, and taking only our electric pocket lamps we crawled along the muddy galleries to No.—.

The noise had stopped, the listener whispered to us when we touched him gently on the leg, so we lay there all three listening for it to start again, the tick-ticking of our wrist-watches and the pulsing of our hearts sounding loud to our strained ears.

Three—five—seven minutes passed by without a sound, and then suddenly there came a slight thud.

The man in front of me stiffened slightly like a well-trained setter and the corporal behind me pinched my leg in the height of his exultation.

The thud-thud continued (there was no mistaking it now), then a pause—and a voice, distinctly guttural, was heard, and a sound, easily distinguishable from the muffled reports of the rifles some thirty feet overhead—the scraping of a shovel on the wooden floor of a gallery not more than eight feet away!

Passing the sentry a revolver and torch, we blew out his candle and crept away as noiselessly as we had come.

On reaching the head of the shaft we met the mining officer, who crawled down and returned to confirm our judgment.

Then followed some mysterious telephoning to the "higher authority" while a charge was hastily laid, and permission was at last secured to "blow" the mine.

No time was lost, and in half an hour all was ready, the mining officer returning from his final inspection with the news that the enemy was still digging blissfully away.

Remembering the mine at Givenchy, we cleared the trench in the danger zone and had this party "stand by to repel boarders" and, if necessary, man the crater.

At 2.30 the mine was fired.

A fountain of earth roared upwards from "No Man's Land," and, armed to the teeth with bombs, we rushed forward, losing a couple of men on the way who had been struck by the falling debris, and manned our trench while machine-guns raked the enemy's parapets.

However, he showed no inclination to man the crater—a yawning pit some forty feet in width half-way over to his trench—and contented himself with throwing a few bombs into it and covering it with machine-gun fire. In spite of which Begbie Lyte, having now risen to the dizzy height of senior subaltern in the company, took out a small party and filled it with barbed wire.

The affair was only briefly mentioned in the *communiques*: "On the 22nd a mine was exploded under a German gallery on our front. An enemy mining party is believed to have been blown up."

The mining officer was greatly pleased, however, as only some few yards of his own gallery had suffered.

CHAPTER 21

Myths, Fairies, Etc.

In every position you take over there are a certain number of myths which when you go out you carefully repeat to the incoming battalion; and the tale seldom loses in the telling. These are handed down to posterity in naming new field-works; hence the frequency of "Suicide Alley," "Sniper's Cross-roads," "Dead Man's Corner," &c, &c.

Some of these myths are worth repeating—all are worth noting, for they are in most cases founded on possibilities.

The most popular myth or fairy on the Messines front was undoubtedly the "Mad Major." This individual was supposed to be an artillery officer who spotted for his own battery—which incidentally always did the most marvellous shooting—from an aeroplane, in which he performed the most daring feats while dodging the "Archibalds" or anti-aircraft shells.

Whether there was any truth in this myth we never found out, but we did see an enemy aeroplane forced down behind our lines by Robert Lorraine, the actor aviator, on October 26th, after a very daring fight.

A large enemy aeroplane of the "Albatross" type had been making a reconnaissance somewhere northward in the Ypres salient with unusual boldness when Lorraine sighted the machine and gave chase. Instead of turning directly back to his own lines the German flew along the line of our trench at such a tempting range that machine-guns all along our line started to cough and spit in the air in an effort to wing him.

Meanwhile our own aeroplane was getting within range, and

a pretty duel in mid-air commenced, the two machines circling and swooping like a pair of immense white gulls, while the "tut-tut" of their machine-guns was the only sound as both Germans and British watched this unique battle.

Suddenly the German machine showed signs of distress, pitched suddenly forward, and started a long glide for the German trenches, our aeroplane still pursuing and forcing the enemy even lower.

But the German had followed our trench line too far down, for at this point our trenches ran forward nearly a quarter of a mile where a French cavalry brigade in a dismounted action the year before had made a last effort to retake Messines.

And now, when it became apparent their machine could not regain the German lines, their gunners began to shell their own plane, containing as it did two of their own men, in an effort to destroy the machine.

But, though they fired over a hundred shells into the little wood behind which the aeroplane landed, they were unable to prevent the men of our Royal Montreal Regiment, who occupied the trenches at this point, from capturing the observer and his papers, the pilot having been killed in mid-air at the time the machine made its fatal plunge.

Then occurred one of the strangest of coincidences, vouched for by the official Canadian Eye-witness, when, on examining the wrecked aeroplane, the Royal Montrealers found the machine-gun with which it had been armed to be one formerly the property of this same regiment, but lost during the fighting around St. Julien just six months before while loaned to another battalion.

The "Mad Major" may have been only a myth, but Lorraine certainly was not, and for this exploit both he and his pilot subsequently received the Military Cross.

But there were a lot of tales that had their origin in a desire to suit the "Cook's tourists." These individuals were officers sent over from the Canadian Training Base for short periods of one or two weeks to receive practical instruction in trench warfare. Incidentally they brought with them some wondrous ideas about the proper methods of doing things, gathered from some official publications known as "Notes from the Front," and were greatly surprised to find we were not in touch with this "trade" journal.

Like the "Daily Summary of Events," known to us as "Comic Cuts" or the "Daily Liar," these little handbooks are written by wise men wearing red tabs and living miles away from the front, where the continuity of their thoughts is only interrupted by the tea hour, and not by the "Jack Johnson" shells. Here they design "wire meat safes," patent refuse burners, mud scrapers, and other weird contrivances that can be fashioned from biscuit tins, ruined houses and other debris, and issue these sheets for the guidance of the poor, long-suffering infantry. Once in a while they turn their attention to steel helmets, grenades, &c., so that their existence is almost justified.

The "Cook's tourist," however, is not a dangerous creature, taken in small quantities, and is a very handy man to send out on working parties when the company is supposed to be resting in reserve. So he is not without his uses.

For those who found the ordinary trench routine dull we had, however, several stock entertainments that never failed to satisfy.

The first and mildest was to take the victim through the "Catacombs," as we called the galleries and connecting passages of our mine. This had the advantage of rendering his cuffs and decorations less conspicuous and giving him in five minutes all the war-worn appearance of a veteran.

If, however, he still craved excitement, he would be allowed to put out some more wire in front of the parapet—always a delicate operation where the lines are close. Many were satisfied by this means.

The third degree was always administered by Captain H- himself. It was in the form of a little sortie from the trench to a stumpy willow in "No-Man's-Land," a willow that bore a striking resemblance to some giant cacti and was called by us the "Cactus Treen."

From this point it was possible to bomb the German trench, and a little excursion of this sort generally satiated the visitor's

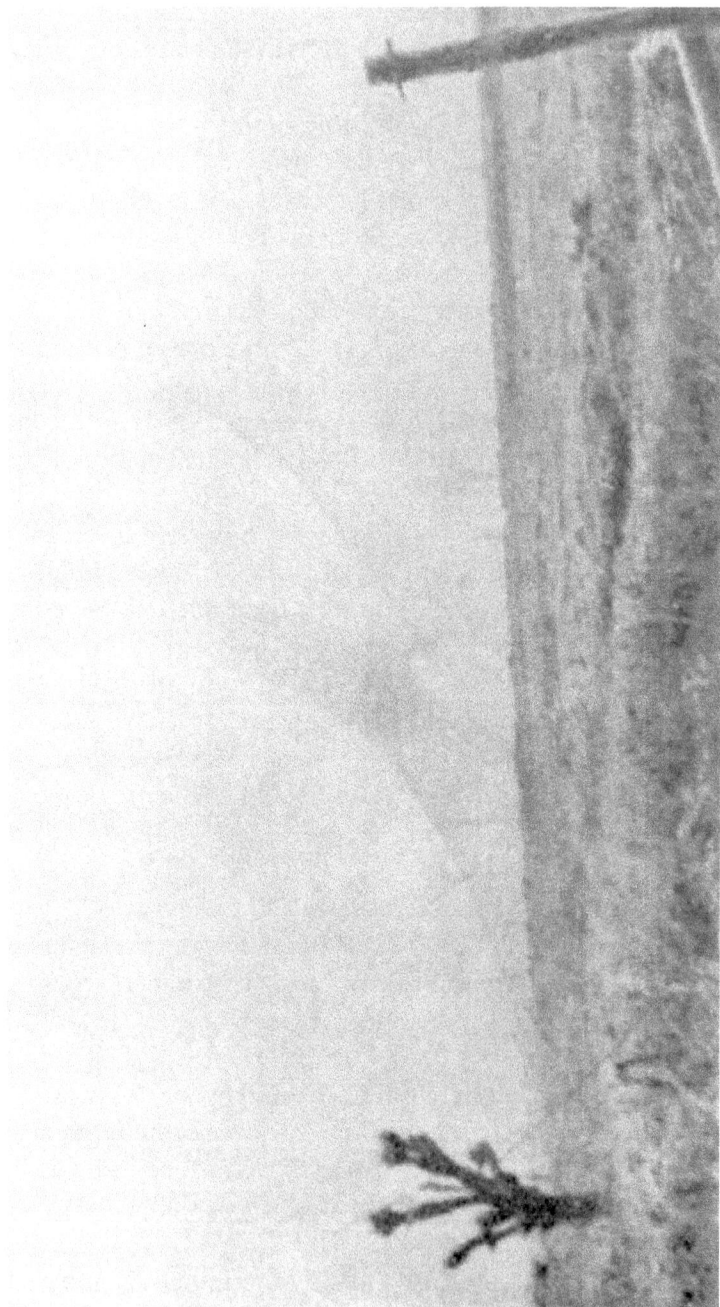

The cactus treen

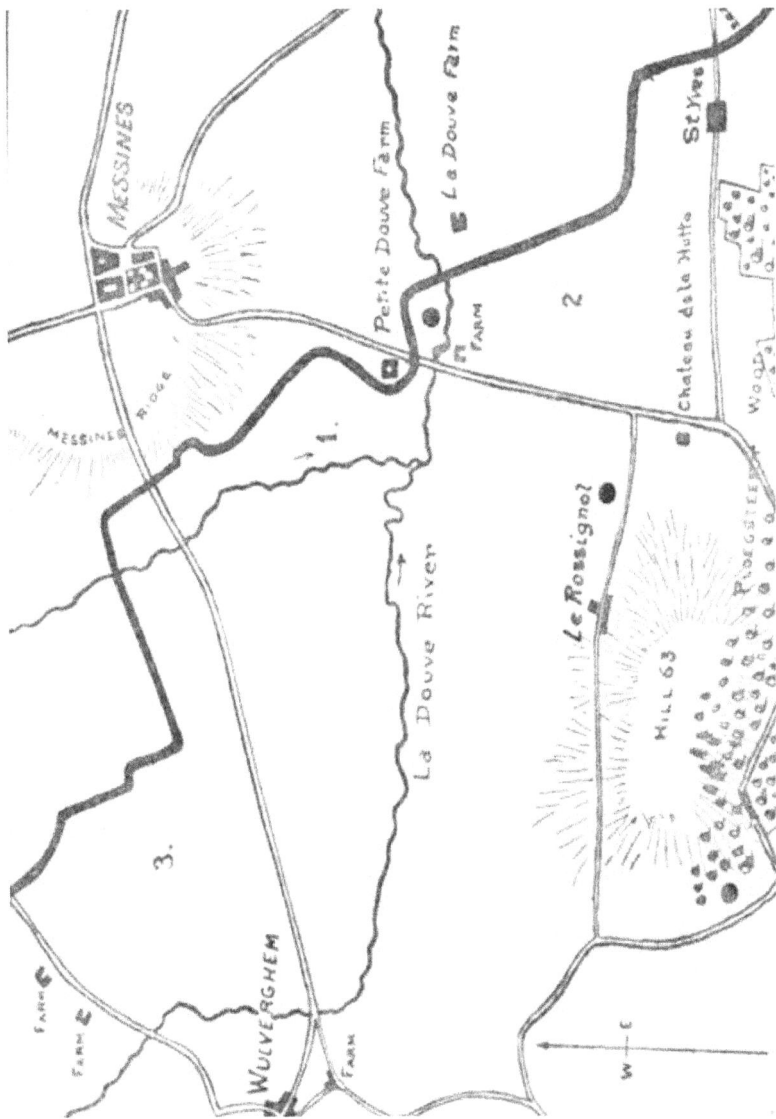

APPROXIMATE GERMAN LINE IN FRONT OF MESSINES DURING WINTER OF 1915–1916
(*Successive positions held by 1st Brigade shown 1, 2, 3.*)

curiosity. Incidentally, it kept the Hun from coming out and bombing us. He did, however, treat us liberally to rifle grenades, and our casualties from these beastly contrivances were large.

On one morning we were most unfortunate, a grenade killing our bombing sergeant and two men, and we started to retaliate with every variety of grenade we had. At this moment the trench mortar officer came up the trench and volunteered to assist us. He had a new gun throwing thirty-pound bombs and was keen on displaying his skill; what was more important, he had twenty bombs available, and he started to fire these off with an alacrity that, under the circumstances, was most pleasing.

But we had reckoned without our host. Before half a dozen rounds had been fired an eight-inch gun back of Messines Hill started searching for the trench mortar man and his gun, and twenty-five high explosive shells plunged around us and shook our trench out of existence. It was very fascinating to watch these shells coming. From the point, high in the air, when they started to drop on their target they could be clearly seen, first as a black ball, then gradually lengthening out till they plunged into the ground and flung up dense fountains of earth and fragments.

The nearest burst was within ten feet of the trench mortar position, and the officer withdrew his party, a sadder and a wiser man.

From the rifle grenades, too, we lost both of our mining officers, one, Lieutenant Alfred Evans, dying of wounds, the other being very severely wounded. So two merry souls who had shared the vicissitudes of our messing passed from our ken, and we could only wait our own fate and say, like the French, *"C'est la guerre!"*

CHAPTER 22

The Winter Months

November brought with it a week of steady rain, and we knew the winter months were at hand. In less than two weeks our trenches, once the pride of the division, were a series of collapsed heaps where the sandbag walls had been undermined by the seepage of water.

But we suffered nothing like the discomforts endured by the British troops during the previous winter. Rubber boots reaching to the thigh were issued, sparingly at first, but gradually until every man had a pair, and whale oil and spare socks were available in large quantities to aid in the fight against trench-foot. Nothing, however, could prevent the mud, which lay a foot deep along the gangways of the trench. Pumps were issued, but the mud was too thick to pump; our only hope lay in drainage, and by the time proper drains were constructed the mud was too thick to run, even though we were on a hill top.

So we pumped and drained and built new sandbag walls all winter, and as fast as one portion of our line was renewed another portion would collapse, or, more disheartening still, be shelled to bits by the big *minenwerfer*.

This was a German gun brought up to this front to counteract our trench mortar. Throwing a shell about six inches in diameter of high explosive, it could in three bursts do more damage than a whole company could repair in a night. And regularly twice a week three shells were dropped along Delta Road, a communication trench forming the third side of the little salient.

The effect of the *minenwerfer* was very local, however, owing

AFTER A FEW SHELLS AND A WEEK'S RAIN

to the thinness of the shell wall, but such men as it killed were not a pretty sight. Fortunately, too, the shells could be seen both by day and night, and rose to such a height before dropping that men could scamper for shelter from the threatened spot. But no dug-out could withstand its explosion, and a series of craters, eight or ten feet in depth and twelve feet in diameter, marked the *minenwerfer's* work.

Every battery that covered our area had, by the time winter was over, reported they had silenced "Minnie," but when we left that area months later she was still doing business at the old stand.

To relieve the monotony of this sort of thing the Canadian Corps organised a series of night raids on the German trenches.

The first, and most brilliant, of these was conducted by the 5th and 7th Battalions of the 2nd Brigade on a barricade or forward trench that had been constructed by the enemy near our old position opposite the Petite Douve Farm.

This raid was made on a villainous night blacker than Egypt during the plagues and raining as only Flanders can.

With faces blackened with charcoal, the raiding parties crept out to the enemy wire and cut it strand by strand, a process lasting several hours. During this time the cooks of one of the battalions carried out pannikins of hot tea to the men who were lying in the mud hacking at the wire.

Finally the path was reported clear except at one point where a deep ditch full of water could not be crossed, and at the appointed moment the raiding parties swooped in on the enemy trench.

Secure, as they thought, on such a vile night, the enemy were completely surprised, but put up a stubborn resistance. An officer and about thirty men were secured as prisoners, and where resistance was more determined the enemy was driven from his trench with bombs. Then on a given signal the raiders returned to their own trenches, bringing helmets, saw-tooth bayonets, and Mauser rifles as souvenirs of their midnight call.

By this time the alarm had spread through the German lines, and his artillery, in response to red signals shot up by men very lately deceased, began to pound their own trench, thus catching their own bombing parties, who, now the trench was only occupied by dead and wounded, had regained the barricade.

But we had another surprise awaiting them. A field-gun had been man-handled up to our front line and at point-blank range proceeded to blow the barricade to bits. This was done and the gun successfully withdrawn by a car from a motor-machine-gun battery, in spite of the fact that the first car sent for this purpose had to be hauled from the ditch into which it had skidded.

So thorough had been the preparations, and so well organised the raid, that an account of it was published in the orders of the French Army as an example of efficient preparation.

The prisoners taken in the Petite Douve affair had boasted of the preparations they were making for a gas attack on a scale hitherto unknown, and on the Sunday before Christmas the enemy made another attempt to gain the Ypres salient by this means.

Early in the morning of the 20th the smell of gas was evident even down as far as our position a few miles south of the salient, and our guns began a desultory bombardment of the enemy lines. Thinking we were as deficient in artillery as in the previous April, the enemy infantry advanced in mass formation about 9 o'clock. Then our artillery did open fire. About noon another attack was made, and also failed without a yard of our line being lost.

There were no further attempts!

On Christmas Eve we were relieved by the Toronto Battalion and marched out to rest billets in divisional reserve.

It was a weird march out. Not a rifle was fired nor a single flare shot up from either trench as the two battalions interchanged.

We wondered if on the morrow there would be the handshaking and hymn-singing that had characterised the first Christmas of the war; a routine order had been published forbidding such demonstrations of good feeling, but it was hardly necessary—flame projectors and asphyxiating gas had attended to that!

Everything was very peaceful in the little hamlet when we arrived, however. It was a clear, starlit night, a little snow in the fields, and the dark silhouettes of the houses and church loomed up against the clear sky. The little church was in darkness—no midnight mass was being sung this year—and we slipped into our various billets in silence, very tired and not a little homesick.

Christmas Day the men were marched into Bailleul, where a big dinner was given them by the officers of the battalion. In the evening another dinner was held for the officers themselves. There were the usual toasts and speeches, and before the party broke up Captain George T. Richardson asked for a few minutes' silent prayer for those who would not be present at our next dinner. It was a wonderful tribute to his sincerity that this was granted, for the evening was well advanced, and soldiers, as a rule, dislike having their religion tampered with by anyone but chaplains and other authorised personages.

Poor George! he was the first of us to go but a few weeks later!

We relieved the Toronto Battalion on the 29th, giving them a chance to celebrate the New Year in a similar fashion.

Then the second week in February we attempted a raid similar to those made on our right and left by other battalions. The most obvious point was selected for the attack, and, by an unfortunate chance, a night when the moon was nearly full.

As a result we were unable to get the wire cut, and the proposed raid was cancelled, the enemy having men dug in amongst their wire watching it.

For some reason or other Captain Richardson, who was in charge of the affair, again went over the parapet, possibly to see that all were safely in, and was discovered a little later fatally wounded in amongst our own wire. He passed away a few hours later in the little dressing station at the Support Farm.

So died a man who never gave a command he would not himself have executed willingly, and whose character and ideals were such that all who knew him envied him.

And on his grave his brother officers placed a wreath with these simple words: "He played the Game."

Epilogue

Our later experiences are too recent for publication today; here, then, this brief story of the Canadians must make an end.

"Crumps"
The Plain Story of a
Canadian Who Went

Louis Keene
Canadian Expeditionary Force

With a Prefatory Note By
General Leonard Wood

Illustrated by the Author

Preface

Headquarters
South Eastern Department
Charleston, S.C.
11th August, 1917

Captain Keene has made an interesting contribution to the literature of the present war in his account of service, which covers the experience of a young officer in the making and on the battle front,—the transformation of an artist into a first-class machine-gun officer. He covers the training period at home and abroad and the work at the front. This direct and interesting account should serve to bring home to all of us an appreciation of how much has to be done before troops can be made effective for modern war, the cost of unpreparedness, and the disadvantage under which troops, partially equipped, labour when they meet highly organized ones, prepared, even to the last detail, for all the exigencies of modern war. It also brings out the splendid spirit of Canada, the Mother Country, and the distant Colonies,—the spirit of the Empire, united and determined in a just cause.

This and similar accounts should serve to make clear to us the wisdom of the admonition of Washington and many others: "In time of peace prepare for war." Many young Americans are about to undergo experiences similar to those of Captain Keene, and a perusal of this modest and straight-forward narrative will help in the great work of getting ready.

Leonard Wood
Maj.-Gen. U.S.A.

The 'Sub'

"Crumps"

The Laurentian Mountains in the Province of Quebec are noted for their beauty, fine hunting and fishing, and are the stamping-grounds for many artists from the States and Eastern Canada. It was in this capacity that I was working during the hot summer of 1914. All through June and July I sketched with my father. Other than black flies my only worry was the price of my tubes of colour. We usually received our newspapers two or three days after publication; consequently we were poorly posted on worldly happenings. Suddenly the war clouds gathered and almost before we knew it they became so threatening that we grew restless, and even went in to the depot to get our papers so that we could have the news sooner.

The assassination of the Austrian Crown Prince and the subsequent events were exciting, but it was only when Russia sent that one word "Mobilize" to Serbia that we suspected serious results. Even the summer visitors from the States exhibited signs of excitement, yet they were sceptical of the chances of war; that is, war that would really affect us! My newspaper in Montreal wired for me to come down to do war cartoons and I left my father and hiked to the depot.

The Montreal train was crowded and conversation centred on the one topic, War; the English Navy's ability to maintain her rule of the seas, and what would Canada do. A young Austrian reservist two seats away was telling some people in a loud voice how much he wanted to get into it. He was going back to answer the call. And I had already begun to hear my country's call.

A newsboy boarding the train at a junction was overwhelmed and succeeded in getting twenty-five cents a copy for his papers.

Montreal teemed with suppressed anxiety and every hour fresh news was posted. Special bulletin boards were put up on store fronts. Already men in uniform were seen in the street. And men were trying to enlist.

The war fever was rising steadily; the chief occupation of Canadians in those days was watching the bulletin boards. Rumours of sea fights, ultimatums, disasters, and victories were common. The Kaiser seemed to declare war on the world at the rate of three countries a day.

On the night of August 4th, as I was putting the finishing touches on a cartoon, a friend burst into the room:—"Come out of here! Something must happen any minute now."

We marched downtown,—everybody marched in those days; walking was abolished in its favour. One met demonstrations everywhere, large crowds of cheering men with flags, victrolas at shop windows played patriotic airs, and soldiers with civilians crowded before the bulletin boards singing the national anthems with great enthusiasm. The King had declared war and his message to the fleet had just been put up! Newspaper extras were given away by thousands and movies of the British Navy were shown on the street. Any one who thought the British could not enthuse, changed his mind then.

The audiences at the theatres and moving picture houses on receipt of the news rose simultaneously and sang the national anthems, then cheered themselves hoarse. These were the first days of the war. Several battalions of militia were called out and posted to protect the bridges and grain elevators. Battalions were raised overnight, and so many recruits came forward that men were refused by the score. England was immediately offered ten battalions. Then an army division was possible. The Militia Department suddenly became a hive of industry. Men with all kinds of business capacity tendered their services gratis, and the Canadian war machine, without the experience of previous campaigns, took shape. They worked night and day bringing everlasting credit on themselves. Banks offered full pay to their

employees in uniform, and this example was widely followed. The principle prompting this action being, "It's our country; if we can't fight ourselves, we will help others to fight for her."

Existent camp sites were inadequate, hence new ones were necessary. We had a few, but none were big enough. We bought Valcartier, one of the best sites in the world, which was equipped almost over-night with water service, electric light and drainage. The longest rifle range in the world with three and one-half miles of butts was constructed. Railroad sidings were put in and 35,000 troops from all over the Dominion poured into it. Think of it,—Canada with her population of seven and one-half millions offering 35,000 volunteers the first few weeks, without calling out her militia. And even today the militia are yet to be called. Thus every Canadian who has served at the front has been a volunteer. England accepted an army division. Fifteen hundred qualified officers were told that they would have to stay and train men for the next contingent. But this was not fighting. They were dissatisfied. They resigned their commissions and went as privates. Uniforms, boots, rifles and equipment were found for everybody. Every man was trained as much as possible in the time allowed, and within six weeks of the declaration of war, guns, horses and 35,000 men were going forward to avenge Belgium.

With me the question of signing up was a big one. In the first place, I wanted to go; I wanted to go quickly. Several other fellows and myself had decided upon a certain battalion. But much to our disgust and regret we were informed that enlistments had stopped only a short time before.

Then came the announcement of the organization of the First Auto Machine Gun Brigade, the generous gift of several of Canada's most prominent citizens, and it was in this unit that I enlisted with my friend Pat, a six-foot, husky Scotchman, with the fighting blood of the kilties very near the surface. We were immediately transported to Ottawa in company with fifty other picked men from Montreal. At Ottawa the complement of our battery was completed upon the arrival of one hundred more men from Ottawa and Toronto. Here we trained until it came

THE CANADIAN

JOHNNIE CANUCK

THE AMERICAN

THE ANZAC

time for us to move to Montreal, and there the battery was embarked on board the *Corinthian* with a unit of heavy artillery. We sailed down to Quebec where we joined the other ships assembled to take over the First Canadian Contingent.

Corinthian
Wednesday, Sept. 30th, 1914.
My Dear Mother and Father:
We are now steaming down the St. Lawrence. No one knows where we are going.

Our fleet is a wonderful sight. All the ships are painted war grey—sides, boats and funnels. We are expecting to pick up the warships which are to convoy us across at Father Point, somewhere near where the Empress of Ireland was sunk.

Quebec looked very fine. The big guns were being hoisted into boats, horses embarking, and battalion after battalion arriving and going aboard. Those who came from Valcartier have had a rough time. They actually look as if they had come through a campaign. It gave me thrills all day to see these fine men come through the dock-gates with a steady swing. It is a magnificent contribution to any army. It's good to think of all these men coming at their country's call.

Some day, if I get back, I want to paint a picture of the fleet assembled at Quebec. The greys and greens looked really beautiful. Quebec, the city of history and the scene of many big battles, views with disdain the Canadian patriotism in the present crisis, and we had no send-off, no flags and no bands.

This letter will not be mailed for ten days, until we are well on the way over. We are crowded, and if we are going through the tropics we shall have a bad time; it is cold now, so we don't notice the congestion.

We had one hundred and forty horses aboard and two batteries of heavy artillery, besides our own armoured cars. All the transports are crowded. We were passed by about ten of the other boats, and as they did so we cheered each other. The thin lines of khaki on all the ships will make a name for themselves. I'm proud I am one of them.

We've had a big dose of vaccine pumped into our arms today. This will be the last letter I send before I arrive, wherever we are going.

The *Corinthian* sailed from Quebec to Father Point, where a patrol boat arrived with orders. We then sailed into the Gulf, but toward evening we turned into the coast. When we passed Fame Point Light a small boat, which afterwards turned out to be another patrol boat, sailing without lights, flashed further orders to us. The *Corinthian* immediately turned round and headed back. The minute the patrol boat's signal light went out we were unable to distinguish it from the sea. The colouring is a good protection; even a boat, close to, sailing without lights, it is impossible to pick out. Apparently our orders were to cruise around until daylight and then sail for the Bay of Gaspe, and this morning at daybreak we sailed into that beautiful, natural harbour, which is big enough to accommodate the entire British fleet.

I expect that to the villagers living around this harbour all events will date from today—today, when the wonderful sight of twenty-five ocean liners drawn up in battleship formation in this quiet place, deserted except for an occasional visit from a river steamer or fishing craft, greeted their gaze.

Five grey fighting ships are mounting guard, and by their signals and pinnaces chasing backward and forward between the troopers are bossing the show. A corporal, a South African War veteran, as we looked at them, quoted Kipling's

The liner she's a lady
With the paint upon 'er face,
The man o' war's 'er 'usband
And keeps 'er in 'er place.

Towards noon a smart launch came alongside. Even at a distance the boys were quick to recognize our popular minister of militia, Sam Hughes, and a thundering cheer rang out. With him were several soldiers who threw bundles of papers aboard.

These were printed copies of his farewell to the troops. His launch sailed by the ship, and then on to the next and so on, through the fleet.

Our orders forbade the display of lights or even striking of matches after 6 p.m.; consequently all lights were masked tonight on the vessels, except those on the *Royal Edward*. The minute her lights were put out the Bay resumed its normal condition, not even the outlines of the vessels being visible.

****

A press photographer on a launch has been taking pictures all the afternoon. Sailed at five o'clock this afternoon just as the twilight commenced. We sailed out in three lines. The convoy is now under way and we extend as far as can be seen in both directions. We have two military police patrols whose chief duty is to see that no matches are struck on deck. Bill, who smokes more matches than tobacco, has had to go below so often to light his pipe, that he has decided to do without smoking on deck. It is surprising how far a match struck in the dark will show. We noticed how matches struck on the other ships showed up last night. All our portholes are screwed down with the heavy weather irons and those of the second-class cabins are covered with blankets. The authorities are taking no chances.

****

We are having physical drills and lectures all day, and we are working just as hard on board as we would ashore. Our speed will not be more than nine knots; the speed of the slowest vessel regulating the speed of the whole fleet.

Matches are getting very scarce. We complained about the tea to the orderly officer today; milk is running out, so the tea is made with milk and sugar in. We asked to have the three separate, but we were told that if we complained we would have all three taken away. As a floor stain it's great, but as tea it's a failure.

We are quartered in the steerage part of the ship and our food is in keeping. It is really remarkable how they can consistently get that same coal-oil flavour in all the food.

****

War news is signalled from ship to ship by semaphore flags by day. It is posted up in the guard room daily. The news that the Indian troops landed in France on the 29th of September was the chief item on the bulletin yesterday. We're short on things to read. Scraps of newspapers are devoured, even to the advertisements. In our cabin we have a "Saturday Evening Post" of September 26th which is thumb-marked and torn, but it is still treasured. We were not allowed to bring anything besides our kit on board on account of the limited space.

Reveille blows at six o'clock and we have to answer the roll-call at 6.15. The idea is, that if the men get up and walk about, they are not so likely to get seasick, but in spite of that quite a number are sick. We have on board one hundred of our brigade; two hundred and sixteen heavy artillery and one hundred and forty horses, together with artillery officers and equipment. The horses take up the same space which in ordinary times is occupied by humans. Otherwise, we should have a great many more troops. Our destination is still a mystery. We're a fleet without a port.

Have just been ordered on fatigue to take a prisoner on deck for exercise. He is to be tried by court-martial tomorrow for striking a sergeant. All day he is kept locked up and only allowed out at night for exercise, under escort. The escort consists of two men and a non-com. While on this job we watched the signallers flashing the war news from the stern of our boat to the bridge of the next astern, the *Virginian*. The news is flashed at night by the lamps—short and long flashes. The news is picked up by wireless on the flagship, the *Charybdis*, at the head of our line and signalled back from ship to ship.

****

This is the list of the fleet. It is written here in the order in which they are sailing. Three warships are heading the fleet; the flagship is the H.M.S. *Charybdis*, commanded by Admiral Wemyss, who distinguished himself a few weeks ago in the Battle of Heligoland.

H.M.S. *Diana*	H.M.S. *Eclipse*	H.M.S. *Charybdis*
Caribbean	*Megantic*	*Scotian*
Athenia	*Ruthenia*	*Arcadian*
Royal Edward	*Bermudian*	*Zealand*
Franconia	*Alaunia*	*Corinthian*
H.M.S. *Glory*	*Canada*	*Ivernia*
Virginian	*Monmouth*	*Scandinavian*
Sasconia	*Manitou*	*Sicilian*
Grampian	*Tyrolia*	*Montezuma*
Andania	*Tunisian*	*Lapland*
Montreal	*Laurentic*	*Cassandra*
Laconia	*Royal George*	H.M.S. *Talbot*

The H.M.S. *Glory*, the vessel on our starboard beam, altered her course today and held up a tramp steamer. We could just see the two vessels through our glasses. Apparently everything was all right as the tramp was allowed to go on her way afterwards.

We are all given our boat stations. This afternoon a submarine alarm was sounded. Everybody on board, including the stewards, had to drop everything and chase to the boats. In the excitement a cook shot a "billy" of soup over an officer's legs, much to our silent delight.

Thinking it over, it will be remarkable if the Germans allow us to cross without making some attempt to sink a few transports. Besides the actual loss of the men, the demoralizing effect it will have on the recruiting would count a great deal. No man likes to be shot or drowned without a show.

****

I am writing this in my cabin, which is only nine feet by six feet and in which six of us sleep at night. Besides living in it we have to keep all our equipment clean, which is some job!

About eleven this morning a commotion occurred in the middle line. The cruiser heading it and the second ship, the *Royal Edward*, turned back. Also several other boats turned in their course. As we have very little excitement we hoped it might be a German attack, for we all want to see a naval battle. I looked at the cruiser through powerful glasses and saw sailors fixing up the starboard lifeboat, so we presumed that it was simply a case of "man overboard."

A big cruiser has joined our fleet and is acting as a flank guard about three miles away from our starboard side.

We have a great deal of physical exercise in spite of the rolling of the deck. This morning, while in the middle of it I was called away to dress and form part of an escort to the prisoner who was to be tried by field court-martial today. The court was very dignified, and it took a long time owing to the inexperience of the officers in such matters. It was the first court-martial I have seen,—the proceedings are strictly legal, being conducted according to the book, and with the officers wearing their swords. The poor devil expects two years.

We have been pitching and tossing a great deal today. Physical exercising on the sloping decks is becoming a mighty risky thing.

Quite a number of the transports have guns mounted on board so they are not entirely dependent on the cruisers. It looks as if we are sailing north of the usual trade routes. I have just heard that five more battleships are on the starboard beam. They came into sight early this morning, but have since been out of sight. We are sailing north of the trade routes.

****

The fleet is being increased. All ships are stopped. Those sailing west are allowed to go after being boarded; those going in the same direction as ourselves are made to fall into line, so there will be no danger of the news of our sailing reaching Europe ahead of us. If we continue to pick up ships sailing in our direction, the fleet will be enormous by the time we arrive at our unknown destination. We sailed two hundred and twelve miles the last twenty-four hours.

Two more transports have joined us. They came from Newfoundland. I hear that we now have forty-three ships in the fleet. We sail at ten cables' length apart, about one thousand yards.

We are getting into more dangerous water evidently. Early this morning the *Royal George* steamed up from the end of the line and took up a position at the head of the fleet, but in line with the battleship *Glory* about three miles away on the port.

The *Laurentic* took up a similar position on the starboard. Both these ships are armoured and have guns mounted on them. They are being used as scouts.

We all rushed up on deck to see a cruiser pass close to us this midday. It was a magnificent sight. She was either the H.M.S. *Bristol* or the H.M.S. *Essex*; her name was painted. The bluejackets were massed on the decks forward and as she went by the marines' band played *The Maple Leaf Forever*. We returned cheers with the sailors. It gives you a great thrill to see a British ship and to have the knowledge of what it represents. To be British is a great thing, and I'm proud to think that I'm going to fight for my country. When this war is over and men are talking round a table, it will be, "Where were you fighting during the war?" not "Did you fight during the war?"

****

I'm in a gun-cleaning squad every afternoon. Today I cleaned the machine gun on which I'm second gunner. We treat our machine guns as if they were pets. No one will ever be able to say that my gun is dirty. It will probably be my best friend some day.

The finding of the court-martial was read out to us on full parade this afternoon. First the "Heavies" were lined up on all sides of the deck, then the "Mosquitos," as the Machine Gunners are called, lined up inside; the prisoner between an escort was led up in the centre. It was wonderfully impressive. I felt that I was to witness the condemning of a fellow soldier to a number of years of hard labour. Over the whole assembly there came a deathlike silence and the finding of the court was read to us by an officer, the sentence being thirty-six days!

The second steward told me that it took two hundred carpenters twelve hours to tear down the cabins and fix up horse fittings. First the authorities made arrangements to ship a thousand troops on this ship. We're crowded as we are now with only three hundred odd. I hate to think what it would have been like with a thousand.

****

Early this morning a large man-o'-war came up on the port at a speed that made everything else seem to stop. We have now battleships on all sides. This ship, although a long way off, looks tremendous. She is one of the latest super-dreadnaughts.

I was on guard last night when one of the cruisers came alongside to *talk* to the captain about having lights showing in some of the ports. I enjoyed it immensely, for I discovered that the British Navy, true to tradition, was still able to maintain its high level of profanity. The ship is in pitch darkness and there is no moon. On deck it's almost impossible to walk it's so dark. Tonight is supposed to be the night on which the Germans are going to make a raid. I am going to sleep on deck so that I shall not miss anything. I'd hate to miss the chance of seeing a naval engagement. I can't see how the Germans can possibly let a chance go by. A cruiser could sink any amount of ships. If the British Navy were up against us they would have had a cut in before now.

Slept on deck last night. Nothing happened except that early this morning a French cruiser joined us, and I got covered with smuts from the smokestack.

The Admiral has received one hundred and twenty-six words of war news, but will not let us have them. Probably they're disastrous. We break up tonight or tomorrow. It's scarcely likely that the whole fleet will be taken to one port at the same time.

That super-dreadnaught passed down the columns today. She is of tremendous size and travels at high speed. She is probably the *Queen Mary*.

Expect to see land Wednesday.

****

Blowing a gale. All day the spindrift has been blowing over. The decks have been too wet for parades, thank God! All the way over we have had physical exercise, sometimes as much as four hours a day. We're all in fine physical condition.

Today we were allowed to wash our clothes. I can see the advantage of khaki now. Even after working hard on my clothes, my underwear is still dark white. The rails were covered with underwear and socks when the storm started. Now every square inch below is used for drying clothes. Even the electric lights are festooned. We have a final kit inspection tomorrow and then we pack for disembarkation. We are only about one hundred miles from the "Bishop's Light."

It has been a very long voyage and we have been very cramped. All our equipment has to be carried in our cabins. Try sleeping six men with all their outfit in a cabin nine feet by six feet. The ship carpenter has a standing job to repair our cabin. We have rough-housed so much that his attention was continually necessary. The trip has been so long that we are now beginning to hate each other. I went down in the stoke-hole and the engine-room. Even amongst the whirling machines it was more peaceful than in our quarters. It seems months since I was in Montreal last.

****

Dear Old England in sight!

We're passing the Lizard now.

The kit has all been inspected and we hope to land tomorrow some time.

We're lying in the historic harbour of Plymouth; arrived here about two hours ago. We're surrounded by fast little torpedo-boat destroyers, which are chasing round us all the time like dogs loosened from a chain. The breakwater has searchlights mounted on each end and fixed lights are playing from the shore. As the lights occasionally flash up the ships in the bay, it is as bright as day. Nobody is allowed ashore, not even the officers. We may go on to Southampton, only we must get there before five at night. After that time nothing is allowed in.

****

Sailed at daybreak on to Devonport. Most of the transports are now lying in pairs at anchor in the harbour. We're close to the shore. We can see naval "jolly boats" and pinnaces sailing back and forth. On one side are lying the H.M.S *Powerful* and another boat, both of which in their day were the pride of the Navy. The *Powerful* was the boat which made such a name for herself in the Boer War. Now both of these vessels are training ships and obsolete so far as this war goes.

All our haversacks have been boiled in coffee to stain them khaki.

One of the Navy steam launches came by and we asked them to get us newspapers. They came back with a bundle and we nearly had a riot trying to get at them.

It was only today that we heard of the fall of Antwerp, the atrocities of Belgium, and the treachery of Maritz in Cape Colony.

We shall be getting off in a few hours and this may be the last I shall write for some time. I have put in a great deal of time during the voyage writing and have done so under difficulties. Sometimes the cabin has been torn in pieces, and often arguments, carried on by leather-lunged opponents of *"Kultur,"* have made this work hard.

We hear that some paper published an account of the sinking of twenty of the ships. This rumour is false, and it's a beastly thing for the newspaper to do, but you must remember to discount all news a great deal.

Still on board and we shall probably be here for a few days more. My, it's galling to be so near to the land and yet to be cooped up in our crowded quarters. Crowded launches and steamers are sailing round the liners. All day long cheering crowds come out to see us. Last night another liner called *Florizel*, with the First Regiment Newfoundland troops, tied up to us. They were a fine-looking lot of men. We told them we had no tobacco; they threw dozens of tins of their tobacco and cigarettes over to us. We fought for them. I got the remains of one tin with most of the contents spilt. Still, as many of us haven't had a smoke for three days, we appreciated it. Several cruisers have come in today, and there seem to be dozens of submarines and torpedo boats cruising around all day. The reason we did not go to Southampton is that five German submarines were waiting for us.

The transports are unloading at the rate of five or six ships a day. It will probably be our turn on Sunday. The fleet looks splendid at night now that we have most of the lights on. All night the steel riveters are at work on three battleships that are being built close by. Near us are several "wooden walls." One is a ship of Nelson's, the *Queen Adelaide*. Every boat, tug, lighter and motor boat here is the property of the Admiralty.

****

We are probably going to Salisbury Plain for two months. We are the first Expeditionary Force to land in England from the dominions or colonies, but others are on their way. The sailors from the training ships serenade us in boats with bands and play *O Canada*, *The Maple Leaf Forever*, and all day long on one ship or the other we hear *It's a Long Way to Tipperary*. Every one is singing it; without doubt it is *the* song of the war. Today we got a bundle of papers. We read them right through to the advertisements. Cigarettes and matches are at a premium and food is running out on board. The strain of staying here is becoming too great. We're all disagreeable and insubordinate. The guard room is already full and will soon need enlarging.

On guard to prevent the men of the two ships (our own and the *Florizel* with the Newfoundlanders) coming over to visit each other. At ten o'clock at night I got the tip that a bunch of men were going to make a break for shore and I was asked to go. I had just come off sentry and was dressed for shore. We all met up forward, hailed a police boat, climbed down a rope ladder across two barges unloading shells and into the police launch. When I got in I found that I and one other fellow were the only privates; all the rest were sergeants and corporals, thirteen altogether, unlucky number. The police sergeants asked me if we had passes. I said, "You bet," and we sailed away from the ship right under everybody's nose. We landed and then took a car to Plymouth and went on the Hoe, which has been in absolute darkness since the beginning of the war. Girls were very interested in us and took most of our collar badges and buttons as souvenirs. One man asked me to give him a cigarette as a souvenir.

We met an English captain in a tobacconist's and he invited us up to the barracks. Two of us went. I was one. To get there we had to go on a street car. We had just sat down when up the stairs came my Lieutenant McCarthy. When he saw me he said, "How the hell did you get here?"

"Oh, just swam across."

"Well, if you get caught it'll be the guard room for you."

I said, "Never mind, we'll have company."

He is a pretty good sport. We went to the barracks, had a session with the captain, then went to the quay, picked up the rest of the men, and sneaked on board. I got to bed at three and had to get up this morning at six o'clock to go on guard.

****

Sunday, very tired. On guard all day, two hours on, four off. It's very unfortunate having a Sunday guard, because in the ordinary way we have to attend church parade in the morning and after having listened to a sermon and sung *Onward, Christian Soldiers*, or, *Fight the Good Fight*, we are free for the day, whereas guards stay on twenty-four hours.

The major noticed one of the sergeants coming on board this morning at six o'clock. The idiot missed us this morning and of course that dished us. The sergeants got in wrong. As I am only a private, and therefore ignorant and simple according to the military code, and, being with non-commissioned officers who are supposed to possess superior intelligence, I got away with it. The sergeants have had to do sentry on the same ladder we went down.

Everybody is as disagreeable as possible. We are lying in midstream and can see the town. Can you imagine anything more galling than that?

While I was on guard the Vicar of Plymouth came aboard and held service. He said that the last time a Vicar of Plymouth preached to warriors was just before Drake sailed to meet the Armada.

Thank God! moving at last. We've moored up to the docks just opposite two magnificent dreadnaughts. Naval men are handling our cargo, our kit bags are packed and we are ready to disembark.

Near our ship's stern is a barge full of ventilators and spare parts of ships which are taken away when ships are cleared for action. Some of the rifle racks were marked *Cornwall* and I noticed a davit post with the name *Highflyer*, the boat that sank the *Kaiser Wilhelm* after she had been preying on the shipping off South Africa. When a ship is cleared for action, all inflammable fittings, such as wooden doors, ladders, racks, extra boats, and davits, etc., are discarded. If the order to "clear the decks for action" comes at sea, overboard go all these luxuries. It is calculated that the cost of "clearing decks" on a cruiser is five thousand dollars.

Some of our stuff was unloaded yesterday, and when the ship moved a guard was placed over it. When the corporal went down the gangplank with the relief, Pat and I walked down behind as if we were part of the same, right by the officers. We had a devil of a job to get through the dock gates, a suspicious policeman and sentry on guard. We told the sergeant of the police a pitiful story, saying that we hadn't had anything to eat for three days, and finally he relented. "All right, my lads, only don't 'swing the lead' in town." We got into Devonport and went to the biggest hotel. Before they had time to throw us out we ordered breakfast of real food. It was fine after the ship's grub. After sitting there ten minutes, the general commanding the district came in and sat behind us. He stared. Two privates in the same room as the general!! But all he said was, "If you boys can fight as you eat, you'll make an impression." Then we visited some other places!

We went back to the docks and went over the super-dreadnaughts, *Tiger* and *Benbow*, the biggest war vessels in the world. The *Tiger's* speed on her trials was 37.5 knots an hour.

After we had seen enough, we went back to the ship and tried to look as if we had been working with one of the fatigue parties on shore. It worked!

We marched off the ship midday and then I had to go on guard again all night. That was the first time we were allowed ashore to see the town, and I was on guard, so if I hadn't slipped ashore on the two occasions mentioned, I should not have seen it at all.

****

It rained all night, and when I was off guard I slept on the top of one of our armoured trucks, under a tarpaulin. It's wonderful how we can sleep now anywhere, and we often have our clothes on for three days at a time. Many a time I sleep with all my equipment on. Get wet and dry it by keeping it on. We all have to do it. The idea of pyjamas or baths as necessities seems funny. At one time I would sooner go without breakfast than miss a bath. Now I make sure of the breakfast.

We are going to drive our cars through England to Salisbury Plain. We started this morning and drove through Devonport. Cheering crowds everywhere. All our cars wear the streaming pennants: "Canada With the Empire," which pleased the people a great deal.

As we rode through the streets people showered gifts upon us, such as cakes, chocolates, newspapers and apples, and everywhere made lusty demonstrations. The people of Taunton, as soon as they heard that the Canadians were coming, turned out the barracks and we were met by all the officers, who came in to talk to us. One second lieutenant, after studying me for some time, said, "Isn't your name Keene?"

"Yes," I replied, "but how do you know?"

"I went to school with you fifteen years ago."

His name was Carter; he was in the Second Dorsets. That night he got me out of barracks for a couple of hours, and we hashed over the schoolboy reminiscences. The people of Taunton were arranging a dance for us, but nobody was allowed to attend. The major believes in putting us to bed early; his theory being that a man can't drive cars well after a party, and he couldn't keep the drivers in alone.

Ladies from Taunton, of the pleasing English type with beautiful complexions, handed round all sorts of rubbish, jam puffs, and other things which belong to the time before we joined the army.

Travelled all the morning. Everybody turned out to see us. The Brigadier-General wired ahead, and hastily prepared placards, still wet, were hanging from the windows—

God Bless the Canadians
Loyal Sons
of the Empire,

The Gathering of
the Lions' Whelps

and in one case the haste was so great that *God Save the King* was hung upside down.

Everybody wants my badges and buttons, and some men in the unit have not one left. Hence I have requisitioned an order for a hundred to meet the demand.

All over the country you see "Kitchener's Army" drilling. In one case we passed about a hundred of them. When they saw us they broke ranks and shook us by the hands. The people of England are much impressed with our speed in coming over. Old men and women shouted, "God bless you, Canadians!" while tears trickled down their cheeks.

I read this notice in one little shop—

At noon every day the church bell will ring a few chimes and everybody is asked to stop whatever he is doing and offer this prayer, *"Oh, Lord, help our soldiers and sailors to defeat our enemies, and let us have Peace."*
(Signed) *The Vicar*

Recruiting notices ten feet by six feet with the sentence *Your King and Country Need You* are to be seen everywhere in shops, on barns, trees, and even church doors.

Motorists and cyclists are warned to pull up whenever requested or the results may be serious. Most of the motors have O.H.M.S. plates above the number plate.

We billeted in a village school; all slept in our blankets on the floor. Left the school and cleaned up before the kids came for their lessons next day.

★★★★★★★★

Salisbury Plain. Arrived today. This part is called Bustard and takes its name from the small Bustard Inn, Headquarters of General Alderson, General Officer Commanding. Troops are here in thousands and we are no novelty. The roads are torn up. Mud is two feet deep in places. All through the day and night motor lorries, artillery and cavalry are travelling over the ground. Aeroplanes are circling overhead and heavy artillery are firing. We see the shells bursting on the ranges every day.

Always raining. Everything is wet, and I am sleeping in a rotten tent which leaks. Still, we are all so fit that what would kill an ordinary man doesn't worry us much.

We all get three days' leave and are trying by every means possible to wangle another day or two. Many men have to see dentists, and lots of men have grandparents in Scotland who display signs of dying suddenly. If the excuse is good enough, we get four days and sometimes five. I have a sweetheart in Scotland, but if that is played out I have to work something else.

****

Wonderful sight from where I am now. Miles of tents, motors and horse lines on this desolate moorland. No houses; only camps and a few trees which have been planted as wind screens. The soil is very poor, too poor for farming. It is government property and it is only used for troops. We are ten miles from a railroad. We are so isolated that we might be in Africa, except that it's so cold.

The papers are starting an agitation to get the Canadians to march through London, and are asking why they should be smuggled in and then shut up on Salisbury Plain. They want to see us, *and we want to see London*!!

Our ambulance car has been used every day since we came here, taking wounded from one hospital to another. The rest of our cars have been used to carry German prisoners.

One of the spies caught on the ships is said to have been shot. Several were arrested; two were caught in Devonport while we were there, one in a Canadian officer's uniform.

****

Am spending seventy-two hours' leave in London. Got leave through this telegram which is from "the girl I'm engaged to":

Disappointed. Met train. Please do come. Leaving for Belgium soon. Love.

Edythe

She is a Red Cross nurse. This is a new one and it worked. McCarthy sent it to me.

London is very dismal. No electric signs, and the tops of all the street lamps are painted black so that the lights don't show from above. However, we managed to have a good time, in spite of it all. The Germans say that the Canadians are being held in England to repel the invasion.

****

The facilities for bathing are not very extensive. I rode into Salisbury, a distance of seventeen miles, yesterday, on top of some packing-cases in a covered transport wagon, for a bath, the first since I was last on leave. We get a Turkish bath in town for thirty cents. After that we had a large juicy steak and then started our seventeen-mile trip back through the pouring rain. Every other mile we got down and helped the driver swear and push the car out of the mud, vast quantities of which abound on the Salisbury roads, believe me!!

****

It is Sunday afternoon. Most of the men in camp are asleep or reading. Outside it is raining. It seems to be always raining, and occasionally we have such a thick fog that even a trip to get water is exciting before you can get back to your own lines.

Owing to our camp having become a swamp we have had to move our quarters to drier ground. Moving the tents is not a big job, but rebuilding the cook-house is! I figure that when I leave the army I shall have a few more professions to choose from. For example, I'm a pretty hefty trench digger; then as a scavenger I am pretty good at picking up tin cans and pieces of paper; also I'm an expert in building things such as shelters from any old pieces of timber that we can steal; then as a cook I can now make that wonderful tea that I wrote you about, besides many other things which we didn't realize that we had to do when we enlisted.

Today the paper says "Fair and Warmer." We could do with some of that. Years ago, before I joined the army and lost my identity, I rather liked occasionally getting wet in the refreshing rain; but now the trouble is that we are always wet and have nowhere to dry our things, except by sleeping on them.

Our major has an original scheme of training men in the ranks to qualify for commissions, sort of having half a dozen embryo officers ready. I have been picked as one and have to study in all my spare time. It means a great deal more work, but it's very interesting and the sort of thing I would like to do. We start today.

****

We began our instruction on the machine gun to the officers and the men who are up here for a special course; I have a boozy lieutenant, who doesn't care a hang, and a bright non-com. Some of the officers we brought over make good mascots.

****

It was fine today. We were even able to open up the tent flap to dry the place a bit. Today the major congratulated me on the Christmas card I designed for the unit.

Our classes of instruction to the "alien" officers finish tomorrow. Both the men I was instructing passed.

The adjutant is very anxious to put us through our officers' training course quickly.

We are now recognized as the specialist corps in the machine-gun work with the Canadian Division, and he is anxious that we shall be ready to take commissions when casualties occur. Every battalion of infantry has a machine-gun section attached, and we have the job of training the officers and sergeants of these sections.

Owing to the bombardment of the east coast, several of our battalions are under orders to move at a moment's notice. It is thought that the bombardment was simply a ruse to draw the British fleet away from around Heligoland.

****

151

The newspaper boys in Salisbury, when you refuse to buy an "Hextra," shout *Montreal Star* and *Calgary Eyeopener*, and all the shopgirls and barmaids in Salisbury say:

"Some kid."

"Believe muh."

"Oh, Boy!"

****

I had been granted Christmas leave at the last minute, and as it was awkward to telegraph to Northwich, I arrived after a long journey, lasting sixteen hours, ten minutes ahead of the letter I'd sent saying I was coming. My arrival soon spread over the town. A Canadian—this was a rather unique thing for Northwich, a little Cheshire town. Out of a population of about eighteen thousand, two thousand men have joined the colours. The men in uniform from the works are all receiving half pay. The other men who are staying are working twelve hours a day and give up part of their pay so that the jobs of the soldiers will be open when they come back. Thirty-five Belgian refugees are being kept here. Money to keep them for twelve months has been subscribed. One huge house has been taken over as a hospital with twenty-three nurses, all volunteers from Northwich. Everybody has done or is doing something in the great struggle. The young ladies in this neighbourhood have no use for a man who is not in khaki, and with customary north of England frankness tell them so.

I expect that you know that the Government has sent around forms to every house asking the men who are going to volunteer to sign, and men long past the military age have signed the papers, "too old for the war service, but willing to serve either at home or abroad voluntary for the period of the war." Others have offered to do work to allow young men to go, to keep their jobs for them. This shows the spirit that permeates England. There is only one end and that *must* be the crushing of the Germans. I don't believe people have any idea of the number of men who are at present under arms, and still the posters everywhere say that we must have more men.

I wonder if you know that the Germans are shooting British prisoners who are found with what they consider insulting post-cards of the Kaiser, and even references to His All Highest in letters are dangerous. As we are nearing the time when we shall go across I thought I would mention it.

We expect to leave England somewhere around January 15th. We have been living in the mud so long that we are getting quite web-footed.

This is a war Christmas. People are too excited and anxious to celebrate it. I wonder what sort of a Christmas the next one will be! What a terrible Christmas the Germans must have had in Germany. They admit over one million casualties. Fancy a million in less than five months. During the Napoleonic wars, which extended over twenty years, six million died, and yet one side in this war already admits one million.

The Canadian ordnance stores have been given instructions that all equipments down to the last button must be ready by the 15th of January. That date seems to be the favourite one. I believe it is the commencement of big things; a move will then be made to embark large numbers of troops across to France.

All our telegraphic addresses were taken when we came away on leave in case it were decided to send units over before our term of leave expired.

A German aviator flew over Dover yesterday and made a fierce and terrible bomb attack on a cabbage patch. Terrible casualty in cabbages. Berlin must have designs on a bumper crop of *sauerkraut*.

****

Back in camp. It was hard to come down to it. Our blankets and clothes left in the tent were mildewed, clammy, and partly submerged. Our feet are wet and we are again soldiers, dirty and cold.

Travelled down in the train with thirty-six men of the Canadian contingent who had formed an escort for fifty-six undesirables who have been shipped back to Canada. It seems strange when men are needed so badly to ship them back because they are a bit unruly or get drunk too often. They will all come back with future contingents. Six of them made a dash for it at Liverpool. Three of them got away altogether.

It snowed yesterday. Last night the camp looked beautiful; the tents lit up through the snow in the moonlight made a pretty picture, a suitable subject for a magazine cover, but mighty uncomfortable to camp in.

****

In a gale last night many tents were blown down. We spent all day putting them up again. The cook house, a substantial frame building, has also blown down again.

When I got back I found a Christmas hamper, a bunch of holly and a small box of maple sugar and packet of cigarettes from the Duchess of Connaught with her Christmas card. All parcels for the troops came in duty free. Our postal system is very efficient. We get our letters as regularly as we would in a town.

People send us so many cigarettes that we sometimes have too many. I wish we could get more tobacco and fewer cigarettes. If you remember during the Boer War the authorities tried to break the "Tommy" of his "fags" by giving him more tobacco. Now they really seem to encourage cigarette smoking, although it really doesn't matter; the same things which are harmful in towns don't have the same bad effects when we are living in the open.

All leave is up by the 10th of January for everybody, officers and men.

The Princess Patricia Canadian Light Infantry have gone to the front to the envy of everybody. It is a splendid battalion with fine officers. They have been lying next to our lines and we have made many friends with the "Pats."

Cerebro-spinal meningitis has broken out, and in spite of all efforts to check it, seems to be gaining ground. Several officers have died with it, and I believe that four battalions are quarantined. We have to use chloride of lime on the tent floors and around the lines. My friend Pat calls it "Spike McGuiness." The worst of a disease like this is that a patient never recovers. Even a cure means partial paralysis for life. I believe that Salisbury Plain is known for it, and I hear that all the ground that troops are now occupying is to be ploughed up when we leave. As far as that goes we have ploughed it up a bit already, but a systematic ploughing will make it more regular. The subsoil is only four inches, then you come to chalky clay. The tent-pegs when they are taken from the ground are covered with chalk.

I think that the Canadian Contingent has had a pretty raw deal. We're not even included in the six army divisions which are going to France by the end of March. Wish I had joined the "Princess Pats," who are already there. We want to fight.

We're having a beastly time as compared with the Belgian refugees and the German prisoners in England. We're beginning to wonder if we are ever going to the front. There is now some talk of billeting us in Bristol. We've been under arms nearly five months and should be good fighting material by now. With a similar number of men the Germans would have done something by this time.

****

All the last week the selected few of us have been working separately on a course of work to qualify us for commissions. We have had to study hard every spare minute when not drilling each other.

Several dogs have attached themselves to us; sometimes they find themselves on a piece of string, the other end being in a man's hand. One of these, a big bull terrier, sleeps in the canteen. The beer is quite safe with him there, but two nights ago the canteen tent, after a great struggle, tore itself off the tent-poles and went fifteen feet up in the air like a balloon, then collapsed. The dog, I regret to say, did not stay at his post, so a quantity of beer will have to be marked down as lost. This same bull has a pal, a white bull terrier, who came out with the officers' class the other morning. We had not been drilling more than fifteen minutes when he came back with a large rabbit. We stewed it at night. It certainly was good.

One of the mechanics has forged an Iron Cross which has been presented to the dog in recognition of his services.

I doubt if I shall ever be able to sit up to a table again regularly. I would much sooner sleep on the floor, and I have found, when on leave, that I preferred sitting on a hearthrug to a chair. Even while writing this I am lying on my blankets. My pipe is burnt down on one side from lighting it from my candle.

****

Today being Sunday and as there were only two of us left in the tent, the others being on leave, we gave it a thorough spring cleaning. It needed it! By some oversight the sun came out to-day, so that helped. We also washed up all our canteens and pannikins with disinfectant.

The infantry are bayonet-fighting and practicing charges every day. If you want a thrill, see them coming over the top at you with a yell; the bayonets catch the light and flash in a decidedly menacing fashion. They practice on dummies, and are so enthusiastic that they need new dummies almost every lesson.

Every man, on becoming a soldier, becomes a man with a number and an identification disk. My number is 45555 and my "cold meat ticket," a tag made of red fibre, is hanging round my neck on a piece of string.

****

We're packing up and expect to go away next week. Of course, it may be another bluff, but somehow I think we really are going now, as we have been fitted out with a "field service-dressing," a packet containing two bandages and safety pins, which we have to sew into the right-hand bottom corner of our tunics. We have also been given our active service pay book, a little account book in which we have our pay entered. We don't get paid much in the field. We carry this book instead.

It seems always cold and wet. We are very hardened. We look tough and feel that way. I haven't had a bath for a month. Since I have been soldiering I have done every dirty job that there is in the army, and there are many. Often when a job seemed to be too dirty and too heavy for anybody else, they looked around for Keene and Pat.

****

"On guard." Writing this in the guard tent, when we are not actually on sentry. We keep all our equipment on, as we are liable to be called out at any minute. We sleep with our belts and revolvers in place.

A quarter guard is three men and a non-com. The men do two hours on and four off. When it comes to a man's turn he has to be on his beat no matter what the weather is like during the day or night. The cold is pretty bad and occasionally it snows. Some units have sentry boxes, but we haven't. We use a bell tent. I was called this morning at five o'clock to do my sentry from five to seven. The small oil stove which serves to heat the guard tents had evidently been smoking for an hour, and over everything was a thick film of lamp-black. Everybody thought it a great joke until they looked at themselves in the mirror and caught sight of their own equipment. We must come off guard as clean as we go on. I got out quickly and left them swearing and cleaning up.

From five to seven is the most interesting relief. I had first to wake the cooks at five o'clock and then I watched the gradual waking up of the camp. At six o'clock I had to wake the orderly sergeants and then far away in the distance the first bugle sounded reveille, then it was taken up all around and gradually the camps all over the Plains woke up. Men came out of the tents, the calls for the "fall in" sounded, and the rolls were called and the usual business of the day commenced. The change from the deadness of the night with its absolute stillness all takes place in a very short time. To a person with any imagination it seems rather wonderful. You must remember that we can see for miles, and in every direction there are hundreds of tents. Each battalion is separate, and they have great spaces between them; still wherever you look you can see tents.

I wonder if I told you that aeroplanes are all the time flying over our camp. With characteristic British frankness they always have two huge Union Jacks painted on the undersides of the wings. We have become so used to them that we scarcely trouble to look up unless they are doing stunts.

****

The frost makes a fine grip for the cars; when the ground freezes over we can take the cars anywhere, but unfortunately it thaws again too quickly. As we are a motor battery we are of course a mile from the road, and sometimes it takes an hour and a half to get on to it.

****

It is a howling night, wind and rain galore. I'm wondering how long the tent will last. I have been out three times already to look at the tent pegs. How often it has been so since we first came on to these plains. If you are living in tents you notice the changes in weather more than under ordinary circumstances, and every rainstorm has meant wet feet for us. But now we have been given new black boots, magnificent things, huge, heavy "ammunition boots," and the wonderful thing is they don't let water in. They are very big and look like punts, but it's dry feet now. I can tell you I am as pleased with them as if some one had given me a present of cold cash. At first they felt something like the Dutch *sabots*. They seemed absolutely unbendable and so we soaked them with castor-oil. Once they become moulded to the feet they are fine. Of course they are not pretty, but they keep the wet out.

We have had new tunics issued to us of the regular English pattern, much more comfortable than our other original ones, and then instead of the hard cap we now have a soft one, something like a big golf cap with the flap on to pull down over the ears. These are much more comfortable. They have one great advantage over the old kind—we can sleep in them. We can now lie down in our complete outfits even to our hats. Once I considered it a hardship to sleep in my clothes. Now to go to bed we don't undress; we put on clothes.

I managed to get a pass to Salisbury on Saturday and went to the local vaudeville show. In the row in front of me were several young officers of the British Army, and it was striking what a clean-cut lot they were. England is certainly giving of her best. They were not very much different from any others, but at the same time they are the type of Englishmen who have done things in the past and will do things again. They are all Kitchener's Army. Thousands of men who have never been in the army before threw up everything to go in the ranks. You see side by side professors, labourers, lawyers, doctors, stevedores, carters, all classes, rich and poor, a great democratic army, drilling to fight so that this may be a decent world to live in.

At present it is almost impossible to use each man in his own profession as they do in Germany, but sometimes the non-commissioned officers work it out in this way.

Sergeant to squad of recruits:

"Henybody 'ere know anythink abart cars?"

"Yes; I do. I own a Rolls Royce."

"Olright; fall out and clean the major's motor bike."

One patriotic mother who had a son who was a butcher did her best to get him to join the Royal Army Medical Corps, because he was proficient at cutting up meat and would feel quite at home assisting at amputations.

****

Now that we are approaching the time for our departure to France we are hearing that favourite farewell to all men going to the front, "Goodbye, I'll look every day for your name in the casualty list."

The "Princess Pats" have already been in action. They had a hard fight and many of them have been put out of business. We envied them when they went away and still do, although it only seems yesterday that we were lying together here and now a number of them are lying "somewhere in France."

The jam-making firm of Tickler was awarded a huge contract for the supply of "Tommy's" daily four ounces of jam; either plum and apple were the cheapest combination or else the crop of these two fruits must have been enormous, because every single tin of jam that went to the training camps, France, Dardanelles, or Mesopotamia, was of this mixture.

We became so tired of it that we used the unopened tins to make borders of flower-beds, or we used them to make stepping-stones across puddles. Eventually the world's supply of plums and apples having been used up, the manufacturers were forced to use strawberries.

In the army all food is handled by the Army Service Corps, and as soon as they found real jam coming through they took it for their own and still forwarded on to us their reserve "plum and apple." The news got around amongst the fighting units: result—the Army Service Corps is now known as the "Strawberry Jam Pinchers."

Reviewed by King George V, and it was indeed a very impressive sight. Although there were only twenty thousand troops, they seemed endless. During the time that the King was on the parade ground in company with Lord Kitchener, two aeroplanes kept guard in the sky. Our K. of K. is a big, fine man who looks the part. An inspection by the King is always a sure sign of a unit's impending departure. He travelled down on the new railway which had just been built by the defaulters of the Canadian Contingent.

At the last minute I managed to get weekend leave and went to London. No Canadians there! I caught sight of a military picket, sergeant and twelve men, looking for stray ones, though. Another picket held me up and made me button my greatcoat. I did! It isn't clever to argue with pickets at any time!

The train was three hours late. Troops' trains were occupying the lines. From Bulford we walked home in a hail-storm. Got in about five o'clock just as the reveille was blowing in the other lines. They were just leaving for the front, and had made great fires where they were burning up rubbish and stuff they couldn't take with them. Tons of it! Chairs, mattresses, and tables. When we move, everything except equipment has to be discarded. We can't do anything with extras. We have to cut our own stuff down to the very smallest dimensions. I walked through the lines afterward of other battalions who had left, and I saw fold-up bedsteads, uniforms, equipment, books, buckets, washing-bowls, cartridges and stoves of every conceivable kind and shape; hundreds, from the single "Beatrice" to the big tiled heaters. Some tents were half full of blankets thrown in, others with harness. All the government stuff is collected, but private stuff is burnt.

In the army you soon realize that you have to make yourself comfortable your own way. I don't hesitate to take anything. If I have on a pair of puttees which are a bit worn and I find a new pair,—well, I just calmly yet cautiously annex them and discard the old ones. We found a barrel of beer had been left by one of the other units, so we carefully carried the prize to our lines and then tapped it. *Zowie!* It was a beer barrel all right, only it was filled with linseed oil.

****

Thank the Lord!! Under a roof, sitting on a real chair; table-cloth, plates; and I'm dry. We have come to Wilton (of carpet fame) and I'm in a billet. I have a real bed to sleep in. Last night I lay on the floor of a mildewed tent; couldn't sleep on account of the cold. Tonight I sleep between sheets, and the wonderful thing is that I'm not on leave.

We drove our cars down here, each of us hoping that we would never again see Bustard Camp, Salisbury Plain, as long as we lived; it had been our home for five months. Yesterday we felt like mutiny; today every one is smiling. As soon as we were "told off" Pat and I went to our billet, a nice clean little house close to the centre of the town. The owner is a baker. I felt kind of uncomfortable with my boots and clothes plastered up with mud, but the good lady said, "Don't 'e mind, come in, bless you; I've 'ad soldiers afore. The last one 'e said as 'ow he couldn't sleep it were so quiet 'ere."

I had a wash (this is Friday night), the first since Wednesday morning. The idea of having as much water as you want, without having to go a half mile over a swamp, pleased me so much that I used about six basinfuls in the scullery.

When the lady of the house asked us *what* we would *like* to eat, we both fainted. I'm afraid we're going to get spoiled here. Couldn't sleep at first. Cold sheets and having all my clothes off—too great a strain! Had breakfast and then drove our cars to the canal, where we scrubbed and washed them down inside and out.

This afternoon I've been into every shop I could find, chiefly to talk to people who are not soldiers. Even went into the church to look around and listened to the parrot-like description of the place by the sexton.

Everybody is happy, and although it has rained ever since we have been here, we haven't noticed it yet. I may say there are four or five kids, and the whole house could be packed into our front room. Still, "gimme a billet any time."

****

I have just received the news that I have been given a Second Lieutenancy in the Motor Machine Gun Service, Royal Field Artillery, and I go into camp at Bisley at once. I am very glad that before being an officer I have been a private, because I now have the latter's point of view. I am going to try hard to be a good officer; promotion always means more work and responsibility—so here goes.

****

I have been very busy lately training my new section, and we are now part of the 12th Battery, Motor Machine Guns, 17th Division British Expeditionary Force, leaving today for the "Great Adventure."

****

Somewhere in France. At last we are here. We landed at a place the name of which I am not allowed to mention, and were then taken by a guide to a "Rest Camp" about two miles from the docks. If they had called it a garbage dump I shouldn't have been surprised. You would be very much surprised with the France of today. Everybody speaks English; smart khaki soldiers in thousands everywhere.

Already I have seen men who have been gassed and the hospitals here are full of wounded. Our troops are arriving all day and night and marching away. English money is taken here, but

French is more satisfactory as you are likely to get done on the change. The officers have a mess here just as in England. Actually we are farther away from the firing line than we were in camp at Bisley; but we leave today on our machines going direct to it. There was a transport torpedoed just outside; they managed to beach her just in time. The upper decks and masts are sticking up above water.

Since I last wrote anything in this diary we have ridden over one hundred and ten miles by road towards the firing line. All day yesterday it poured. The country was beautiful, ripening corn everywhere, the villages are full of old half-timbered houses, the roads are all national roads built for war purposes by Napoleon, and run straight; on either side are tall, poplar shade trees, so that the roads run through endless avenues.

At night we stayed in a quaint village inn. The men all slept in a loft over their machines. Our soaked clothes were put in the kitchen to dry, but owing to the number of them, they just warmed up by the morning. One officer has to follow in the rear of every unit to pick up the stragglers. I had to bring up the rear of the column today—result: I didn't get in until early in the morning, only to find the other subalterns "sawing wood."

****

Yesterday was the French National Day. We were cheered as we rode along, and women and children smothered us with flowers. In the morning a funeral of two small children passed us. Our battery commander called the battery to attention and officers saluted. The priest was two days overdue with his shave—soldiers notice things like that, you know.

****

Today we continued our ride; the weather was much better—dried our clothes by wearing them. Strange to run through Normandy villages and suddenly come across British Tommies—many of them speaking French. A Royal Navy car has just passed us; our navy seems omnipresent. I saw an old woman reading a letter by the side of an old farmhouse to some old people, evidently from a soldier, probably their son. It reminded me a great deal of one of Millet's pictures. Every one thinks of the war here and nothing but the war; it's not "Business as Usual."

We stay here one night and move away tomorrow. We can hear the guns faintly.

The three section officers, myself and two others, are sleeping in a hut together. It is one of these new collapsible kind, very convenient. We are now all in bed. Outside the only sound we can hear is the sentries challenging and the mosquitoes singing.

****

All males are soldiers in France, even the old men. They look very fine in their blue uniforms, but I have a prejudice for our khaki Tommies. We get good food as we travel, but pay war prices for it. Cherries are now in season; we don't pay for them, however.

****

Rode another sixty miles today. A car smashed into the curb, cannoned off and ran over me, busting my machine up. The front wheel went over my leg. My revolver and leather holster saved me from a fracture, but I got badly bruised up. I was very scared that I should not be able to go "up" with the Battery. It would be almost a disgrace to go back broken up by a car without even getting a whack at the Boche. Had to ride later on another machine twenty-five miles through the night without lights, in a blinding rain.

****

Everything interesting. Should like to have a camera with me. I had to post mine back. So many things are done in the British Army by putting a man on his honour. They just ask you to do things. They don't order you to do it. It was that way with me; they merely "asked" me to post my camera back.

Great powerful cars rush by here all day and all night, regardless of speed limits. Every hour or so you see a convoy of twenty or thirty motor lorries in line bringing up ammunition or supplies, or coming back empty. Every point bristles with sentries who demand passes. If you are not able to answer satisfactorily, they just shoot. The French soldiers have magnificent uniforms; the predominating colour is a sort of cobalt blue. To see sentries, French and British together, they make quite a nice colour scheme.

Officers censor all letters. I censor sometimes fifty letters a day. One man put in a letter today, "I can't write anything endearing in this, as my section officer will read it." Another, "I enclose ten shillings. Very likely you will not receive this, as my officer has to censor this letter." Of course we don't have time to read all the letters through. We look for names of places and numbers of divisions, brigades, etc., but I couldn't help noticing that one of my men, whom I have long suspected of being a Don Juan, had by one mail written exactly the same letter to five different girls in England, altering only the addresses and the affectionate beginnings.

The village in which I am now was visited last September by twelve German officers who came through in motor cars; the villagers cried, *"Vivent les Anglais,"* for not having seen an English soldier they took it for granted that the "Tommy" had come.

Everybody goes armed to the teeth. I have my belt, a regular Christmas tree for hanging things on, with revolver and cartridges on even while I'm writing this. We carry a lot, but we soon get used to it.

****

The corn is being cut now. Through the window opposite I can see it standing in newly-stacked sheaves. These places are the favourite sketching grounds of artists in normal times, and I often wonder if they ever will be again.

We return salutes with all the French and Belgian officers. It is difficult sometimes to distinguish them. I got fooled by a Belgian postman, and then went to work and cut a French general.

The nearer we get to the firing line the finer the type of soldier. They are the magnificent Britishers of Kitchener's First Army. It makes you proud to see them marching by, dirty and wet with sweat. I watched two battalions come through; they had marched twenty miles through the sun with new issue boots; a few of them had fallen out, and other men and officers were carrying their equipment and rifles; many of the officers carried two rifles.

I am now well within sound of the guns. A German Taube was shelled as it came over our firing line yesterday. One man was lying on his back asleep with his hat over his eyes, when a piece of shrapnel from one of the "Archies" hit him in the stomach—result: one blasphemous, indignant casualty. From the road I can see one of the observation balloons, a queer sausage-shaped airship. We may be moved up into the thick of it at any time now.

****

I have been over into Belgium today: crossed the frontier on my motor bike; the roads are terrible, all this beastly "pave" cobblestones; awful stuff to ride over on a motor cycle. Shell holes on both sides of the road, and I saw three graves in the corner of a hop garden. All along the road there were dozens and dozens of old London motor buses, taking men to the trenches. They still have the advertisements on them and are driven by the bus-drivers themselves. Three hundred came over with their own machines. They are now soldiers. The observation balloon I mentioned yesterday was shelled down today.

I am writing this in an old Flemish farmhouse, and the room I'm sitting in has a carved rafter ceiling, red brick floor and nasty purple cabbage wallpaper. All the men of the house with the exception of the old man are at the war; one son has already died. The Germans have been through here. They tied the mayor of the town to a tree and shot him. The trenches have been filled in, all the wreckage cleared, and they have a new mayor.

****

It is not yet 7 a.m. I am an orderly officer and have to take the men out for a run at six. I came back and bought a London *Daily Mail* of yesterday from a country-woman. We are at least three miles from the town, but they are enterprising enough to bring papers to us at this time in the morning. A *Daily Mail* costs four cents.

166

Since I last wrote I have been up to the front line. Everything is different from what you imagine. The German trenches are easily distinguished through glasses; their sand-bags are multicoloured. Shrapnel was bursting over ruins of an old town in their lines. When you look through a periscope at the wilderness, it is difficult to imagine that thousands of soldiers on both sides have burrowed themselves into the earth. The evidence of their alertness is shown by their snipers, who are always busy whenever the target is up.

A battery of eight-inch howitzers was opening fire. Our battery commander, hearing this, sent us up. The guns, big fellows, were well concealed. They were painted in protective colours and covered with screens of branches to prevent aerial observation. In the grounds all over the place were dug-outs, deep rabbit burrows, ten or twelve feet down, into which everybody went immediately. The Germans started their "hate." The firing is done by hand cord; other big guns are fired electrically. An enormous flash, an ear-splitting crash, a great sheet of flame from the muzzle, and two hundred pounds of steel is sent tearing through the air to the *"Kultur"* exponents. The whole gun lifts off the ground and runs back on its oil-compression springs. These guns are moved by their own caterpillar tractors which are kept somewhere close by. In three quarters of an hour they can get them started on the road. The ground for these emplacements was the orchard of a chateau. While we were there a whistle blew three times, an order shouted; immediately the guns were covered up and the men took cover. The enemy had sent an aeroplane to locate them. If they could once find them, hundreds of shells would rain on this spot in a few minutes. At a few yards' distance I couldn't see the guns myself. The "Hows" were firing at a house in the German lines which had been giving trouble. In three rounds they got it and then started in to "dust" the neighbourhood. Of course, the firing is indirect. The officers and men who are with the guns don't see the effects. Apparently they fire straight away in the air. The observation is done by the forward observing officer in the fire trenches who corrects them by 'phone.

After the appointed number of rounds had been fired, we adjourned to the chateau, a fine house, marble mantelpiece, plaster ceilings, gilt mirror panels, etc. It has still a few pieces of furniture left, no carpets, most of the windows are smashed; shells have visited it, but chiefly in splinters. I saw one picture on the wall with a hole drilled in by a shrapnel bullet which had gone clean through as though it had been drilled. It hadn't smashed the glass otherwise. From a window of the room, which the officers use as a mess, a neat row of graves is to be seen. Outside there are great shell holes, most of them big enough to bury a horse. Suddenly a shriek and a deafening explosion occurred in the garden. "Sixty-pound shrapnel! Evening hate," said an artillery sub. We left! We had been sent up to see the guns fire and not to be fired at.

To go home we had to pass a village completely deserted, a village that was once prosperous, where people lived and traded and only wanted to be left alone. Now grass is growing in the streets. Shops have their merchandise strewn and rotting in all directions. On one fragment of a wall a family portrait was still hanging, and a woman's undergarments. A grand piano, and a perambulator tied in a knot were trying to get down through a coal chute. To wander through a village like this one that has been smashed up, and with the knowledge that the smashing up may be continued any time, is thrilling. Churches are always hateful to the Germans. They shell them all; bits of the organs are wrapped around the tombstones, and coffins, bones and skulls are churned up into a great stew. In some of the villages a few of the inhabitants had stayed and traded with the soldiers. They lived in cellars usually and suffered terribly. British military police direct the traffic when there is any, and are stationed at crossroads with regular beats like a city policeman.

While travelling to another part of the line we had an opportunity of seeing the "Archies" (anti-aircraft guns) working. They were mounted on lorries and fire quite good-sized shells. They fired about fifty shots at one Taube, but didn't register a bull. Later in the evening from a trench we had the satisfaction of seeing another aeroplane set on fire, burn, and drop into the

German lines like a shot partridge. Aeroplanes are as common as birds. Yesterday a "Pfeil" (arrow) biplane came right over our lines and was chased off by our own machines. The enemy's aeroplanes have their iron cross painted on the underside of their wings and are more hawkish-looking than ours. They are more often used for reconnoitring and taking photographs than for dropping bombs.

We are being moved up closer to the firing line. I have been made billeting officer. I went to headquarters; a staff colonel showed me a subdivision on a map. "Go there and select a place for your unit." The place was a wretched village of about six houses, all of which are more or less smashed about, windows repaired with sacking and pieces of wood. All of the inhabitants have moved except those who are too poor. Every square inch is utilized. I managed to get a cow-shed for the officers. It looks comfortable. On the door I could just decipher, written in chalk, by some previous billeting officer—

2 Staff Officers
6 Officers
2 Horses

Billeting chalk marks are on almost all the shops and houses up from the coast to the front.

The field which we are expecting to put the men into belonged to a miller who lived in a different area. We went to see him. He couldn't speak English or French, so I tried him with German. While we were talking, I noticed some non-coms watching us very intently and was not surprised to find one following us back down the road. When he saw our car he came up and apologized for having taken us for spies. They are looking for two Germans in our lines wearing British uniforms, who have given several gun positions away. Two days ago the enemy shelled the road systematically on both sides for half a mile when an ammunition column was due. It was quite dark before we left; the sky was continually lit up by the star shells, very pretty white rockets, which light up No Man's Land. The enemy has a very good kind which remains alight for several minutes.

Our days of comfortable billets are over, I am afraid. Unless you are working hard, it is miserable here,—wrecked towns, bad roads, shell holes, smells, dirt, soldiers, horses, trenches. The inhabitants are a poor, wretched lot. Many of them are thieves and spies. We are right in Belgium, where flies and smells are as varied as in the Orient.

Wherever we travel by day or night we are constantly challenged by sentries and have to produce our passes. We stopped in one darkened shell-riddled town and knocked up an *estaminet*; we got a much finer meal than you can get at many places farther back. We talked to the woman who kept it and asked her if she slept in the cellar.

"Oh, no! I sleep upstairs, they never bombard except at three in the morning or nine at night. Then I go into the cellar."

This woman was a very pleasant, intelligent person, most probably a spy. Intelligent people generally leave the danger zone.

Marching through the sloughed-up mud, through shell holes filled with putrid water, amongst most depressing conditions, I saw a working party returning to their billets. They were wet through and wrapped up with scarves, wool helmets, and gloves. Over their clothes was a veneer of plastered mud. They marched along at a slow swing and in a mournful way sang—

"Left—Left—Left We—are—the tough Guys!"

Apparently there are no more words to this song because after a pause of a few beats they commenced again—

"Left—Left—Left—"

They looked exactly what they said they were.

Windmills, of which there are a good many, are only allowed to work under observation. It was found that they were often giving the enemy information, using the position of the sails to spell out codes in the same way as in semaphore; clock-hands on church towers are also used in the same way.

I saw a pathetic sight today. A stretcher came by with a man painfully wounded; he was inclined to whimper; one of the stretcher-bearers said quietly to him, "Be British." He immediately straightened himself out and asked for a "fag." He died that night.

****

We had a terrific bombardment last night; the ground shook all night and the sky was lit up for miles. The Boches used liquid fire on some new troops and we lost ground.

I found this piece of poetry on the wall of a smashed-up chateau, and I have copied it exactly as I found it. The writing was on a darkened wall, and while I copied it my guide held a torchlight up to it. The place passes as "Dead Cow Farm" on all official maps.

I've travelled many journeys in my one score years and ten,
And oft enjoyed the company of jovial fellow men,
But of all the happy journeys none can compare to me
With the Red-Cross special night express from the trenches to the sea.

It's Bailleul, Boulogne, Blighty, that's the burden of the song,
Oh, speed the train along.
If you've only half a stomach and you haven't got a knee,
You'll choke your groans and try to shout the chorus after me.

Bailleul, Boulogne, and Blighty, dear old Blighty 'cross the sea.'

Now some of us are mighty bad and some are wounded slight,
And some will see their threescore years and some won't last the night,
But the Red Cross train takes up the strain all in a minor key
And sings Boulogne and Blighty as she rumbles to the sea.

Oh, it's better than the trenches and it's better than the rain,
It's better than the mud and stink; we're going home again,
Though most of us have left some of us on the wrong side of the sea.
We are a lot of blooming cripples, but—downhearted? No, siree.

There's a holy speed about this train for each of us can see
That we will cross the shining channel that lies 'twixt her and me
To the one and only Blighty, our Blighty, 'cross the sea,'
Where the blooming Huns can never come, 'twixt her and
*   home and me.*

"Blighty" is the wound which sends a man home to England; it's a war word which came originally from the Indians, but now universally adopted in the new trench language.

I was walking along a trench when a man, who was sitting on a fire-step looking up into a little trench mirror (which is used by putting the end of the bayonet between the glass and the frame), just crumpled up, shot through the heart. He didn't say a word. The trench had thinned out and the bullet had come through, nearly four feet down from the top of the parapet.

Bad shell fire this afternoon. Saw shells churning things up seventy-five yards away; many passed overhead; had a ride on my motor cycle with the other officers to reconnoitre the roads leading down to the part of the trenches we have taken over; road was shelled as we came along. Two "coal boxes" hit the road and smashed up a cottage in front of us; we picked up pieces of the shell too hot to hold.

Our billet now is another large farm, with the pump in the centre of the manure heap as usual; our machines are parked all round a field close to the hedges to make a smaller target and also to prevent aerial observation.

I went through a town this morning which has been on everybody's lips for months—I have never seen such devastation in my life; it baffles description. The San Francisco earthquake was a joke to this. Thousands and thousands of shells have pummelled and smashed until very little remains besides wreckage. Most of the shelling has been done to deliberately destroy the objects of architectural value.

My quarters are in a loft amongst rags, old agricultural implements, sacks, and the accumulation of years of dirt; flies wake me up at daylight.

This morning I went for a drink in the *estaminet* I have mentioned already. Two shells have been through the sides of the house since we were last there, but they both came through at the usual scheduled time.

This poor country is pockmarked with shell craters like a great country with a skin disease. Trees have been splintered worse than any storm could do. Nothing has been spared. The mineral rights of this territory should be very valuable some day. When we have all finished salting the earth with nickel, lead, steel, copper, and aluminium, old-metal dealers will probably set up offices in No Man's Land.

Belgium will have to be rebuilt entirely, or left as it is, a monument to *"Kultur."*

****

My section has been ordered up to a divisional area on the south of the salient. In accordance with instructions I went up to Ypres this morning to find a place to park the machines. Contrary to the popular belief, we do not fight our guns from the motor cycles themselves. We use our machines to get about on, and the guns are taken up as near as possible to the position we are to occupy, which is usually behind Brigade Headquarters. Brigadiers have a great aversion to any kind of motor vehicle being driven past their headquarters, owing to the movement and noise, which they believe attracts attention to themselves, and as a rule the sentries posted outside will see that no machines go by. We get up as far as we can, because after we part from our machines, everything must be carried up through the trenches by hand.

I arrived at the town early and reported to the major who is in charge of the town and of the troops quartered there. He was living in the prison, a substantial brick and stone building, which has been smashed about a bit, but which is still a fairly good structure. The major is a fine, gruff old gentleman who was a master of fox hounds in the North of England. He came over with a detachment of cavalry. He is past the age limit, and it was decided that although he was a fine soldier, perhaps his age would be a deterrent and his job ought to be something lighter, so they gave him one of the fiercest jobs in the world—O. C. Ypres!

I was sent in, and when he heard my errand he said, "You want to park your machines in Ypres? Why don't you take them up in the German front lines? You'll be safer there than here. Listen to the shelling now." I knew this, but I was doing just exactly what I was told. He continued: "I have now thousands of troops here and my daily casualties are enormous, so naturally I don't want any more men. The best plan for you will be to go down the Lille road and pick a house below 'Shrapnel Corner.' "

Bringing Up A Motor Machine Gun

I went on through the town, under the Lille gate, across the tram lines, past the famous cross-roads known as "Shrapnel Corner" and chummed up with some artillery officers. They told me that I could have any of the houses I wanted. I picked a couple which looked to me to be more complete than the rest and chalked them up. This whole place was alive with batteries. While I was there I heard a shout and suddenly a hidden battery of guns, sunk behind the road with the muzzles almost resting on it, started firing across in the direction of the part of Belgium occupied by Fritz. I had passed within two feet of these guns and yet had not seen them, they were so well "camouflaged." On my way back I saw the "Big Berthas" bursting in the town, and I was surprised that so little damage had been actually done to the Lille gate itself. Shells had visited everywhere in the neighbourhood, but had not smashed this old structure.

I went home, collected my men together, and told them the importance of the work we were to undertake. I have found it always a good thing to make the men think the job that they are doing is of great importance. Better results are obtained that way.

We went to an "engineer dump" on the way up just after the enemy had landed a shell on a wagon loading building material, and wounded were being carried off and the mangled horses had been dragged on one side. As the wounded came by I called my section to attention, the compliment due to wounded men paid by units drawn up.

We drew our sandbags in the usual way by requisitioning for five thousand and getting one thousand. Always ask for more than you expect to get.

As we came into Ypres, a military policeman on duty told me it was unhealthy to go the usual way through the Market Square, because the shelling was bad in that part of the town, so I spread the machines out and started on down a side street. We were getting on finely and I was congratulating myself on getting through, when two houses, hit from the back, collapsed across the street in front of my machine. Without any ceremony I turned my machine back along the street which we had come and went through the Market Square down the Lille road, under the gate, being followed by my section. About four hundred yards down I stopped; holding my solo motor cycle between my legs, standing up, I looked back. I counted my machines as they came up. If it hadn't been so scary, it really would have been funny, to see these machines coming down the road through shell holes and over piles of bricks, as fast as the drivers could make them go. The men were hanging on for dear life and the machines rocked from side to side, but they were all there.

Down the road we went to the houses; there we parked the machines and unpacked. A guard was placed over them and the rest of us marched down to the trenches.

****

An officer has to buy all his own equipment and is allowed two hundred and fifty dollars by the Government towards the cost. An officer carries a revolver, but all junior officers as soon as possible acquire a rifle. The men of a "salvage company" were collecting all the rifles, bayonets, and parts of equipment near where I was today and I managed to get a Lee-Enfield (British rifle) in good shape. I felt that I would like to have a rifle and bayonet handy. I found a good-looking bayonet sticking in the side of a sandbag wall. It looked lonely. The scabbard I am using was resting in a loft of a deserted brewery. I am now complete with rifle, bayonet, and scabbard.

Sometimes you see a man smashed about in a terrible way, such a mess that you think he is a goner; he may recover. Another man may have just a small wound and will die. A bullet hitting a man in the head will smash it as effectually as a sledge-hammer. Once a man leaves your unit, wounded, you don't see him again. You get a fresh draft.

No one thinks of peace here. Germany must be put in a similar state to Belgium first.

We never travel anywhere without our smoke helmets; they come right over our heads and are tucked into our shirts; they have two glass eye-pieces. When we have them on we look like the old Spanish gentleman who ran the "Star Chamber." Helmets must always be ready to put on instantly. Gas is a matter of

"Wipers"

seconds in coming over. The helmets are better than respirators, but have to be constantly inspected. A small hole, or if one is allowed to dry, means a casualty.

Storm brewing. Flies bad, driven in by the wind. Nature goes on just the same. I suppose that this farm would be just as fly-ridden in an ordinary summer. During the bombarding yesterday I noticed swallows flying about quite unconcerned. Corn, mostly self-planted, grows right up to the trenches. Cabbages grow wild. Communicating trenches run right through fields of crops; flowers grow in profusion between the lines, big red poppies and field daisies, and there are often hundreds of little frogs in the bottom of the trenches.

****

A trip to No Man's Land is an excursion which you never forget. It varies in width and horrors. My impression was similar to what I should feel being on Broadway without any clothes—a naked feeling. Forty-seven and one half inches of earth are necessary to stop a bullet, and it's nice to have that amount of dirt between you and the enemy's bullets. The dead lie out in between the lines or hang up on the wire; they don't look pretty after they have been out some time. It's a pleasant job to have to get their identification disks, and we have to search the bodies of the enemy dead for papers and even buttons so that we can know what unit is in front of us. Flowers grow in between, butterflies play together, and birds nest in the wire. When the grass becomes too high it has to be cut, because otherwise it would prevent good observation. In some places grass doesn't have a chance to even take root, let alone grow. The shells take care of that.

I managed to get a translation of a diary kept by a German soldier who fell on the field. Below is an exact translation and gives the point of view of a man in the trenches on the other side of the line. He was writing his diary at the same time I was writing mine, and we were both fighting around the salient at Ypres, Hooge being on the point of the salient farthest east. This part, which was once a place of beauty which people came

178

long distances to see, is now like a great muddy Saragossa Sea which at the height of its fury has suddenly become frozen with the tortured limbs of trees and men, and wreckage and reeking smells, until it can again lash itself in wild fury into whirlpools. It is in all respects Purgatory, but of greater horror than Dante ever dreamt of.

****

DIARY OF F— P— OF THE 6TH COMPANY,
3RD BATTALION, 132ND REGIMENT
KILLED AT HOOGE ON AUGUST 9TH, 1915

On *May 10*, we were told to prepare for the journey to the front. Each man received his service ammunition and two days' rations, and we then started with heavy packs on our backs and our water-bottles full of coffee. After a long march we reached our reserve position, where we were put into rest billets for two days in wooden huts hidden in a wood. We could hear from here the noise of the shells coming through the air.

On *May 13*, we moved into the trenches, in the night. We were a whole hour moving along a communication trench one and one-half metres deep, right up to the front line some fifty metres from the enemy. This was to be our post. We had hardly got in before the bullets came flying over our heads. Look out for the English! They know how to shoot! I need hardly say we did not wait to return the compliment. We answered each one of their greetings and always with success, inasmuch as we stood to our loop-holes for twenty-four hours with two-hour reliefs.

At length early on the 15th, at four o'clock, came our first attack. After a preliminary smoking-out with gas, our artillery got to work, and about ten o'clock we climbed out of the trenches and advanced fifty metres in the hail of bullets. Here I got my first shot through the coat. Three comrades were killed at the outset of the assault, and some twenty slightly or severely wounded, but we had obtained

179

our object. The trench was ours, although the English twice attempted to turn us out of it.

The fight went on till eleven o'clock that evening. We were then relieved by the 10th Company, and made our way back along the communication trenches to our old positions. Here we remained until the third day, standing by at night and passing two days without sleep. We were hardly able to get our meals. From every side firing was going on, and shots came plugging two metres deep into the ground. This was my baptism of fire. It cannot be described as it really is—something like an earthquake, when the big shells come at one and make holes in the ground large enough to hold forty or fifty men comfortably. How easy and comfortable seemed our road back to the huts.

We remained in the huts for three days, resting before we went up again to "Hell Fire," as they call the first line trenches in front of Ypres.

Then suddenly in the middle of the night an alarm. Our neighbours had allowed themselves to be driven out of our hard-won position, and the 6th Company, with the 8th and 5th, had to make good the lost ground. A hasty march through the communication trenches up to the front, the night lit up far and wide with searchlights and flares and ourselves in a long chain lying on our bellies. Towards two in the morning the Englishmen came on, 1500 men strong. The battle may be imagined. About 200 returned to the line they started from. Over 1300 dead and wounded lay on the ground. Six machine guns and a quantity of rifles and equipment were taken back by us, the 132nd Regiment, and the old position was once more in our possession. What our neighbours lost the 132nd regained. There was free beer that evening and a concert! At 11 p.m. once more we withdrew to the rear, our 2nd, 4th and 10th Companies relieving us. We slept a whole day and night like the dead.

On *June 15th*, we again went back to rest billets, but towards midday we were once more sent up to the front line to reinforce our right wing, which was attacked by French and English. Just as we got to our trenches we were greeted by a heavy shell fire, the shells falling in front of our parapets, making the sandbags totter. Seeing this, I sprang to the spot and held the whole thing together till the others hurried up to my assistance. Just as I was about to let go, I must have got my head too high above the parapet, as I got shot in the scalp. In the excitement I did not at once realize that I was wounded, until Gubbert said—"Hullo, Musch! Why, you're bleeding!" The stretcher-bearer tied me up, and I had to go back to the dressing-station to be examined. Happily it was nothing more than a mere scalp wound, and I was only obliged to remain on the sick-list four days, having the place attended to.

June 24th. All quiet in the West, except for sniping. The weather is such that no offensive can take place. The English will never have a better excuse for inactivity than this—"It is raining." Thank God for that! Less dust to swallow today! Odd that here in Belgium we are delighted with the rain, while in Germany they are watching it with anxiety.

Today we shall probably be relieved. Then we go to Menin to rest. Ten days without coming under fire. It is Paradise!

Sunday, June 27th. At nine o'clock clean up. At eleven roll-call. At three o'clock went to the Cinema—very fine pictures. In the afternoon all the men danced till seven, but we had to take each other for partners—no girls.

July 2nd. 11 p.m. Alarm. Three persons have been arrested who refused to make sandbags. They were pulled out of bed and carried off. Eight o'clock marched to drill. This lasts till 11. Then 1 to 4 rest. Six, physical drill and games. I went to the Cinema in the evening.

July 6th. Inspection till eleven. Three hours standing in the sun—enough to drive me silly. Twenty-three men fell out. Three horses also affected by the heat. Eleven to one Parade march—in the sun. Thirty-six more men reported sick. I was very nearly one of them.

July 9th. Preparation for departure. From seven to ten pack up kits. Eleven, roll-call. One-thirty, march to light railway. At seven reached firing trench. The English are firing intermittently over our heads; otherwise, all is quiet. We are now on the celebrated, much-bewritten-about "Hill 60." Night passes without incident.

July 12th. At three in the morning the enemy makes a gas attack. We put on respirators. Rifle in hand we leap from the trenches and assault. In front of Hill 60 the enemy breaks, and we come into possession of a trench. Rapid digging. Counter-attack repulsed. At nine o'clock all is quiet, only the artillery still popping. This evening we are to be relieved. The 132nd Regiment is much beloved by the English! In a dugout we found two labels. One of them had the following writing on it: "God strafe the 132nd Regiment (not 'God strafe England' this time). Sergeant Scott (?) Remington, Sewster Wall (?)." On the other was, "I wish the Devil would take you, you pigs."

At 7.20 Hill 60 is bombarded by artillery, and shakes thirty to fifty metres, as if from an earthquake. Two English companies blown into the air—a terrible picture. Dugouts, arms, equipment—all blown to bits.

July 17th. Marched to new quarters. We have got a new captain. He wants to see the company, so at 8 a.m. drill in pouring rain. Four times we have to lie on our belly, and get wet through and through. All the men grumbling and cursing. At eleven we are dismissed. I, with a bad cold and a headache. I wish this soldiering were all over.

July 19th. At seven sharp we marched off to our position. Heavy bombardment. At nine we were buried by a shell. I know no more. At eleven I found myself lying in the

Field Hospital. I have pains inside me over my lungs; and headache, and burning in the joints.

July 20th. The M.O. has had a look at me. He says my stomach and left lung are suffering from the pressure which was put on them. The principal remedy is rest.

July 21st. Thirty-nine degrees of fever (temp. 100 deg. Fahr.). Stay in bed and sleep, and oh! how tired I am!

July 22nd. I slept all day. Had milk and white bread to eat.

July 26th. Returned to duty with three days' exemption, i.e., we do not have any outdoor work.

July 28th and 29th. Still on exemption. Nothing to do but sleep and think of home and of my dear wife and daughter. But dreaming does not bring peace any sooner. How I would love an hour or two back home.

July 31st. In rest. Baths going. Duke of Wuerttemberg passed through our camp.

August 1st. Up to the trenches. Shrapnel flying like flies. A heavy bombardment; bombardment of Hooge. Second Battalion, 132nd Regiment, sent up to reinforce 126th Regiment, which has already lost half its men.

August 4th. Heavy artillery fire the whole night. The English are concentrating 50,000 Indians on our front to attack Hooge and Hill 60. Just let them come, we shall stand firm. At three marched off to the front. Watch beginning again. Five o'clock marched off to the Witches' Cauldron, Hooge. A terrible night again. H.E. and shrapnel without number. Oh, thrice-cursed Hooge! In one hour eleven killed and twenty-three wounded and the fire unceasing. It is enough to drive one mad, and we have to spend three days and three nights more. It is worse than an earthquake, and any one who has not experienced it can have no idea what it is like. The English fired a mine, a hole fifteen metres deep and fifty to sixty broad, and this "cauldron" has to be occupied at night. At present it isn't too badly shelled. At every shot the dug-outs sway to and fro like a weather-cock. This life we have to stick to for months. One needs nerves of steel and iron. Now I must crawl into our hole, as trunks and branches of trees fly in our trench like spray.

August 6th. Tonight moved to the crater again, half running and half crawling. At seven a sudden burst of fire from the whole of the artillery. From about eleven yesterday fires as if possessed. This morning at four we fall back. We find the 126th have no communication with the rear, as the communication trenches have been completely blown in. The smoke and thirst are enough to drive one mad. Our cooker doesn't come up. The 126th gives us bread and coffee from the little they have. If only it would stop! We get direct hits one after another and lie in a sort of dead end, cut off from all communication. If only it were night. What a feeling to be thinking every second when I shall get it!—has just fallen, the third man in our platoon. Since eight the fire has been unceasing; the earth shakes and we with it. Will God ever bring us out of this fire? I have said the Lord's Prayer and am resigned.

****

Today I saw the "Mound of Death" at Saint-Eloi; it has been mined a number of times, and thousands of shells have beaten it into a disorderly heap of earth; the trenches are twenty-five yards apart; all the grass and vegetation has been blown away and never has had time to grow up again.

It's all arranged for you, if there's a bit of shell or a bullet with your name on it you'll get it, so you've nothing to worry about. You are a soldier—then be one. This is the philosophy of the trenches.

****

War is a great ager. Young men grow old quickly here. It can be seen in their faces; they have lost all the irresponsibility of youth. I have met many men who have been here since Mons;

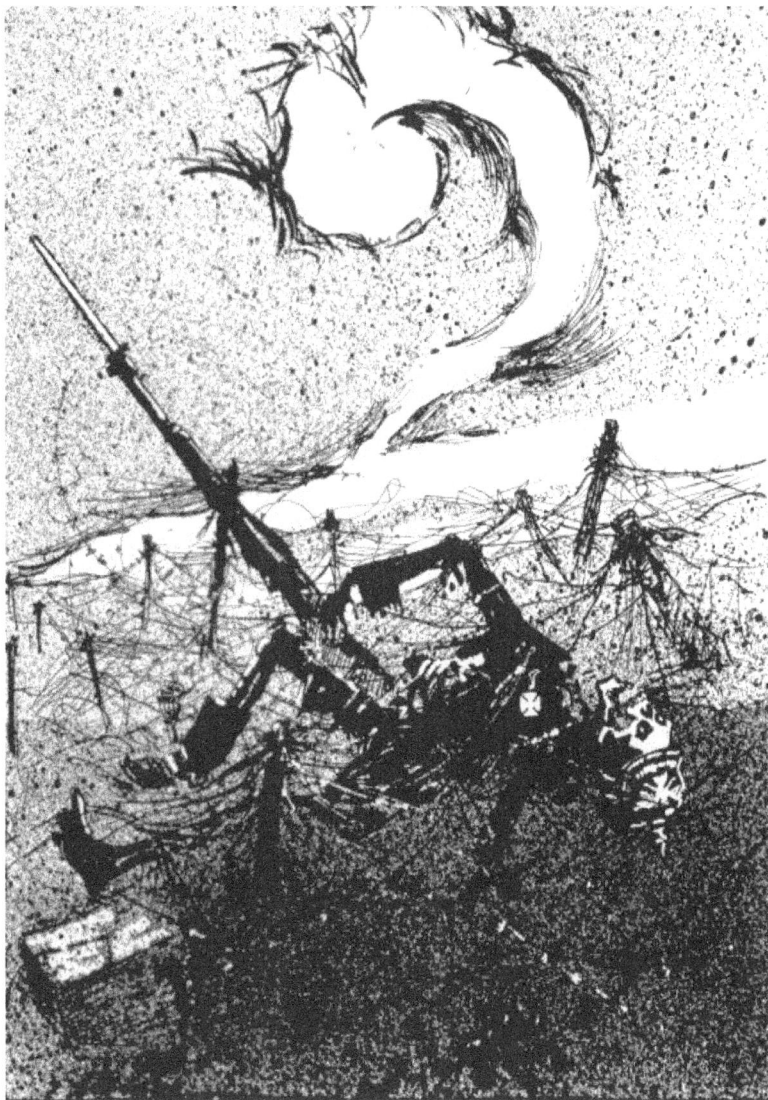

WHAT'S THE USE?

they all look weary and worn out by the strain. Now new troops are coming forward and it is hoped that they will be able to send some back for a rest.

Several days ago the adjutant of the Tenth Battalion Sherwood Foresters came to me with this message which was sent through our lines:—

****

Arrest Officer Royal Engineers with orderly. Former, six feet, black moustache, web equipment, revolver. Latter, short, carries rifle, canvas bandolier. Please warn transports and all concerned.

****

Everybody kept a good lookout for these spies. One sentry surprised a real R.E. officer named Perkins who was working out a drainage scheme. Seeming to answer the above description, he stalked him,—"Come 'ere, you ——, you're the —— I've been looking for." The officer, nonplussed, commenced to stutter. "Sergeant, I've got 'im and he can't speak a word of English." The sergeant collected him in and guarded him until another engineer officer, known to the guard, came along. As soon as Perkins saw him, he said, "F-r-r-ed, t-t-tell this d-d-damn fool wh-ho I am."

"Who the hell are you calling Fred? I don't know him; hold him, sergeant, he's a desperate one." Scarcely able to contain his joy, Fred went back to the Engineers' Camp to tell the great news and Perkins spent three hours in the sandbag dugout listening to a description of what the sergeant and his guard would do to him if they only had their way.

The real spies, who did a great deal of damage, were finally rounded up and shot in a listening post trying to regain their own lines.

****

Enemy snipers give us a great deal of trouble. It is very difficult to locate them. One of our men tried out an original scheme. He put an empty biscuit tin on the parapet. Immediately the sniper put a bullet through it. Now thought the Genius, "If I look through the two holes it will give me my direction,"—so getting up on the fire-step he looked through, only to roll over with the top of his head smashed off by a bullet. The sniper was shooting his initials on the tin.

****

We are all used to dead bodies or pieces of men, so much so that we are not troubled by the sight of them. There was a right hand sticking out of the trench in the position of a man trying to shake hands with you, and as the men filed out they would often grip it and say, "So long, old top, we'll be back again soon." One man had the misfortune to be buried in such a way that the bald part of the head showed. It had been there a long time and was sun-dried. Tommy used him to strike his matches on. A corpse in a trench is quite a feature, and is looked for when the men come back again to the same trench.

We live mostly on bully beef and hard tack. The first is corned beef and the second is a kind of dog biscuit. We always wondered why they were so particular about a man's teeth in the army. Now I know. It's on account of these biscuits. The chief ingredient is, I think, cement, and they taste that way too. To break them it is necessary to use the handle of your entrenching tool or a stone. We have fried, baked, mashed, boiled, toasted, roasted, poached, hashed, devilled them alone and together with bully beef, and we have still to find a way of making them into interesting food.

However, the Boche likes our beef. He prefers the brand canned in Chicago to his own, and will almost sit up and beg if we throw some over to him. The method is as follows: Throw one over ... sounds of shuffling and getting out of the way are heard in the enemy trench. Fritz thinks it's going to go off. Pause, and throw another. Fritz not so suspicious this time. Keep on throwing until happy voices from enemy trenches shout, "More! Give us more!" Then lob over as many hand grenades as you can pile into that part of the trench and tell them to share those too.

It takes some time to distinguish whether shells are arrivals or departures, but after a while you get into the way of telling their direction and size by sound. Roads are constantly shelled, searching for troops or supply columns. I was coming home today, up a road which ran approximately at right angles to main fire trenches. At one place the road was exposed for a matter of thirty or forty feet, and again farther up it was necessary to go over the brow of a small hill. This was about three hundred yards farther on and was exposed to the enemy's view. Thinking they wouldn't bother about a single rider on a motor cycle, I went up past the first exposed position. My carburettor was giving me some trouble and I thought I would see if any rain had got into it, so I turned off the road down a cross-road and dismounted when *crash!* a shell landed right in the middle of the road as far up the exposed place as I was round the corner. Then five more followed the first shell. Had I gone on I could not possibly have missed collecting most of the fragments. The German gunners had spotted me in the first position and decided that a lone man on a motor cycle must be either an officer or despatch rider. So they tried to get him. The shells were shrapnel and the time was calculated splendidly. They had taken into consideration the speed of my motor cycle. Cross-roads are particularly attended to, for there is a double chance of hitting something, and in consequence it is always unhealthy to linger on a crossroad.

****

Dugouts are often made very comfortable with windows, tiled floors and furniture taken from neighbouring shattered chateaux. I have even seen them with flowers growing in window-boxes over the entrance. They all have names. Some I saw yesterday were called "Anti-Krupp Cottage,"

"Pleasant View," and "Little Grey Home in the West." There was one very homey site, well equipped and fitted, which had been dubbed the "Nut,"—the colonel lived there.

My old corps brought an aeroplane down with a machine gun last night. They were in a shell hole between the main and support trenches.

For the last few days I have been "up" looking for gun positions.

The lice are getting to be a torment. You have no idea how bad they are. Everybody up here is infested with them. I have tried smearing myself with kerosene, but that does not seem to trouble them at all. Silk underwear is supposed to keep them down. I suppose their feet slip on the shiny surface.

The food lately has taken on a wonderful flavour and I now know how dissolved German tastes. The cook, instead of sending back two miles for water to cook with, has been using water from the moat in which a Boche had been slowly disintegrating.

Today I was able to see what a German seventeen-inch shell could do; one had made a crater fifty feet across and twenty feet deep in the middle of the road. The top of the road was paved— think it over—and pieces kill at a thousand yards. Thirty horses were buried in another hole.

****

I have been given a special job by the general to enfilade a wood over the Mound. I have my section now in the second-line trenches waiting till it is dark before making a move. We have to make a machine-gun emplacement in a piece of ground which is decidedly unhealthy to visit during daylight. I have been there in daylight, but I had to creep out of it. On the map it is called a farm, but the highest wall is only three feet six inches high.

****

Arrived home about two o'clock this morning. We crawled to the place we have to take up, and I put some men filling sandbags in the ruins and others even digging a dugout. The enemy had "the wind up" and were using a great number of star shells. When one goes up we all "freeze," remain motionless, or lie still. They send them up to see across their front, and if they locate a working party, then they start playing a tune with their machine guns. Bullets and shells whistled through the trees all the time. They seemed to come from all directions. The men didn't like it at all. I wasn't altogether comfortable myself, but an officer must keep going. I walked about and joked and laughed with them. The range-taker said, "Some of us are getting the *didley-i-dums*, Sir."

I don't know what that is, but I had a feeling that I had them too.

Of course, to start with, everybody thinks every single shell and bullet is coming straight for him. Then you find out how much space there is around you. One man came to tell me that two men were firing at him with his own rifle from the ruins of the alleged farmhouse, ten yards away from the dugout we are making. Just then a field mouse squeaked, and he jumped up in the air and said, "There's another." I told the men to fill sandbags from the ruins; they all crowded behind this three-foot-six wall for protection; they dug up a French needle bayonet—that was all right, but they afterwards dug up a rifle and I noticed a suspicious smell, so I moved them.

We came home very tired. We are attacking Hooge, a counter-attack, to take back trenches lost in the liquid fire attack— you will hear what we did from the papers, probably in three months' time.

****

I'm writing this in a new home, this time a splinter-proof dugout. The Huns are again strafing us—last shell burst fifty yards away a few minutes ago. Several times since I started writing I have had to shake off the dust and debris thrown by shell bursts on to these pages. I was again sniped at with shrapnel this morning on my machine while reconnoitring the roads—they all missed, but they're not nice. I'm filthy, alive, and covered with huge mosquito bites; you get sort of used to the incessant din in time. Even the forty-two centimetre shells, which make a row like freight trains with loose couplings going through the air, are not so terrible now.

Through a hole in my dugout I can see the Huns' shells *Kulturing* a chateau. It was once a very beautiful place with a moat, bridges, and splendid gardens. Now it's useless except that the timber and the furniture come in useful for our dugouts and the making of "duck walks," the grated walks which line the bottom of the trenches.

Last night I was sitting in the Medical Officer's dugout when a man I knew came in. He was an officer in the Second Gordons. "I feel pretty bad, doc." He explained his symptoms. "Trench fever; you go down the line."

"No, fix me up for tonight and maybe I won't need anything else." He didn't! All that is left of him is being buried now, less than a hundred yards from where I write this.

****

Before I came here I had to go to another part of the line, in which the "Princess Pats" distinguished themselves. We have been hanging on ever since, and a mighty stiff proposition it is. The O.C. today told me that he had not slept for fifty-six hours. The Germans in one place are only twenty-five yards away—so close that conversation is carried on in a whisper.

In one place they had stuck up a board with *Warsaw Captured* on it.

My section worked until two o'clock and then the sandbags gave out, so we had to come home. This was a disappointment to me. I wanted to get the job finished. My men went on filling sandbags from the same place last night and discovered the remains of the late owner of the sword bayonet. He has now been decently buried, with a little wooden cross marked—

To an Unknown French Soldier R.I.P.

When you read in the newspapers, that a trench was lost or taken, just think what it means. Think what happens to the men in the trenches; that's the part of it we see. Stretchers pass by all day. Since I have been here the cemetery has grown—a new mound—a simple wooden cross. Nobody talks about it, but everybody wonders who's next. The men here are splendid, the best in the world, and the officers are gentlemen.

****

We have moved to the famous Langhof Chateau on the Lille road. This is supposed to have belonged to Hennessey of "Three Star" fame, but the Germans had been through the wine cel-

A French Soldier.

lars. We looked very, very carefully, but only found empties. My batman has made me comfortable. I'm writing this on a wash-stand; in front of me I have a bunch of roses in a broken vase. My trench coat is hanging on a nail from a coat-hanger. A large piece of broken wardrobe mirror has been nailed up to a beam for my use. One of the men just came in to ask if a trousers press would be of any use. We have a fine little bureau cupboard of carved oak; we use this for the rations. A pump, repaired with the leather from a German helmet, has been persuaded to work and has been busy ever since. The roof of my cellar is arched brick and has a few tons of fallen debris on the floor upstairs. That strengthens it. It is shored up from inside with rafters. This makes the roof shell-proof, except for big shells, and the enemy always use big shells. The cellar floors are concrete.

It is very strange the lightness with which serious things are taken by men here, and it took me some time to understand it. I met a young captain of the Royal Marine Artillery who was in charge of a battery of trench mortars. He was telling me of how one of his mortars and the crew were wiped out by a direct hit. He referred to it as though he had just missed his train.

Two days later I went up with the Machine-Gun Officer of the Second Gordons to look at a piece of ground. To get there we had to crawl on our hands and knees. In one part of our journey we came to a sunken road. The day was fine, so we lay there. He asked me about Canada. He wanted to know some-thing about the settler's grant. He said: "Of course you know after a chap has been out here in the open, it will be impossible to go back again to office life." I boosted Canada and suddenly the irony of the situation occurred to me. Here we were lying down in a road quite close to the German lines, so close that it would be suicide to even stand up, and yet here we were calmly discussing the merits of Canadian emigration. I commented on this and he replied: "My dear fellow, when you have been out as long as I have, you will come to realize that being at the front is a period of intense boredom punctuated by periods of intense fear, and that if you allow yourself to be carried away by depression it will be your finish." He had been out since just after Mons.

I remembered this and I found that the nonchalant and carefree attitude of the average British officer was really a mask and simulated to keep his mind off the whole beastly business: this great big dirty job which white people must do.

I was sitting one afternoon by the side of the canal bank about two hundred yards in front of my chateau having tea with the officers of the East Yorks when suddenly the chateau-smashing started again. To go back was dangerous and useless. My men were under cover, resting, so that they would be ready for the night work. The shelling was intermittent. One shell went over and presently I heard *crack,—crack,—boom, crack, crack,—crack*; my heart was in my boots and I was unable to move.

The colonel listened for a few seconds, then said: "Keene, do you know what that is?" I lied: "No, sir." I thought it was the explosion of my machine-gun bullets in their web belts and I dreaded to go up to see my section. I had worked with them and tried hard to be a good officer and the feeling that I should probably only find their mangled remains sickened me. The colonel said: "That's the 'Archie' in Bedford House. I think the last 'crump' got it. You two"—indicating myself and another officer—"go up and see if we can do anything. See if they want a working party and let me know."

We started to run. On the way up I looked into the cellars to see the men whom I, the minute previously, had mourned for, and found two asleep, three hunting through their shirts, and the rest breaking the army orders by "shooting craps." From Bedford House a long trail of smoke was rising and the explosions became louder. We suddenly discovered the "Archie" in flames. It was in the courtyard and for camouflage had been covered with branches. It was mounted on an armoured Pierce-Arrow truck. The "crump" had hit it, and gasoline, paint, branches, and hubs were supplying the fuel which was cooking out the ammunition, the *crack, crack*, being the report of single shells, whereas one loud *boom* signified the explosion of an entire box. These shells were going off in all directions and it became dangerous to stay too near.

The flames on the car were of pretty colours. It is surprising the amount of inflammable material there is on a car. The late owner of the car, a lieutenant in the Royal Marine Artillery, was cursing in a low, but emphatic, marine manner, and several other officers from nearby batteries were attracted by the noise and the pyrotechnic display. I spoke to the lieutenant and sympathized with him, and he retorted: "*Gott strafe* Germany. Why they should hit the 'bus' when I have a brand-new pair of trench boots that I had never worn, I dunno." Just then and there the case cooked out and a piece of shell cut between us and buried itself deep in the support of a dugout, so we got under cover.

In the group was a splendid type of army chaplain. He came over almost at the start of the war and had seen a great deal of the open warfare at the commencement of hostilities. He said: "My friend Fritz is not through; he'll try to do some more yet." As the smoke died down and the cracking stopped, the enemy decided that an attempt would be made either to carry out salvage of whatever they had hit or else we would try to get the wounded away. So without any preliminary warning the whole area was covered by a battery fire of *whiz bangs*, and the shrapnel bullets came down like rain, several men being hit. The fire eventually died down and the wreck was allowed to cool off. The "Archies" are used so much to keep the aeroplanes up, and next to the loss of his boots the officer in charge was worried by the fact that the enemy would send an aeroplane over to see what they had hit. It was very necessary to keep the planes away, because at this time there were one hundred and fourteen batteries of artillery in the neighbourhood.

Later on the battery commander came down, and as he looked at the red-hot armour plates he said: "Five thousand pounds gone up in smoke. Sorry I missed the fireworks." The Divisional general called him up at the dugout and gave him areas for the distribution of the four anti-aircraft guns and cars comprising his battery. After he was through the commander replied: "Very good, sir, that will be done with all the guns except the third gun." The voice over the wire became very dignified, a preliminary to becoming sulphuric. "What do you mean, all but the third gun?"

Whiz-Bangs

"Because, sir, the enemy has just 'crumped' the third gun and all that remains of it is scrap iron."

One of the battalions has a fine victrola in the officers' mess dugout with a good selection of records. I have heard Caruso accompanied on the outside by an orchestra of guns. It was a wonderful mixture. Speaking of canned music reminds me we have a small portable trench machine, which closes up like a valise, easily handled and carried about. One man near had a box full of needles distributed in his back by a bomb; he considers himself disgraced; he says it will be kind of foolish in years to come to show his grandchildren twenty-five or thirty needles and tell them that they were the cause of his wounds.

The Tommies play mouth organs a great deal and it is much easier to march to the sound of one, even

'Ere we are; 'ere we are,
'Ere we are agin.
We beat 'em on the Marne,
We beat 'em on the Aisne,
We gave 'em 'ell at Neuve Chapelle,
And 'ere we are agin—

sounds well with the addition of a little music.

Anything is used for trench work; often if we waited for the proper materials we should be uncomfortable, so it is one of the qualifications of a good soldier to find things. Sometimes we steal material belonging to other units, then stick around until the owners come back and help them look for them; however, it is always advisable to steal materials from juniors in rank; if they find it out, and are senior, then you are in for a one-sided strafe.

One of the other battery subalterns found a deserted carpenter's shop and he let his men loose to dismantle it. They took the parts of steel machines and used them for the construction of a dugout. One man said, "It's like coming home drunk and smashing up the grand piano with an axe."

They must have attracted the attention of the ever-alert Boche, for no sooner had they moved out than the place was shelled to the ground. Everything I now look at with an eye to its value for trench construction; thus, telegraph poles, doors, iron girders, and rails are more valuable to us out here than a Rolls Royce.

****

Slang or trench language is used universally. My own general talks about "Wipers," the Tommy's pronunciation of Ypres, and I have seen a reference to "Granny" (the fifteen-inch howitzer) in orders "mother" is the name given to the twelve-inch howitzer. The trench language is changing so quickly that I think the staff in the rear are unable to keep up to date, because they have recently issued an order to the effect that slang must not be used in official correspondence. Now instead of reporting that a "dud Minnie" arrived over back of "mud lane," it is necessary to put, "I have the honour to report that a projectile from a German Minnenwerfer landed in rear of Trench F 26 and failed to explode."

Sometimes names of shells go through several changes. For example, high explosives in the early part of the war were called "black Marias," that being the slang name for the English police patrol wagon. Then they were called "Jack Johnsons," then "coal boxes," and finally they were christened "crumps" on account of the sound they make, a sort of *cru-ump!* noise as they explode. "Rum jar" is the trench mortar. "Sausage" is the slow-going aerial torpedo, a beastly thing about six feet long with fins like a torpedo. It has two hundred and ten pounds of high explosive and makes a terrible hole. "Whiz bang" is shrapnel.

Shelling is continuous. We have thousands of pieces of shells and fuse caps about the premises. I have in front of me a fragment of a shell about fourteen inches long and about four and one-half inches across, which came from a German gun. The edges are so sharp that it cuts your hand to hold it. I use it as a paper-weight.

****

This morning I experienced a wonderful surprise. I had gone up to one of the North Stafford Batteries to borrow a clinometer. The major, while he was getting the instrument for me, casually remarked: "There's yesterday's *Times* on the bench if you care to look at it."

The "Crump."

I turned first to the casualty list and later to the *London Ga-zette* for the promotions, and wholly by accident perused carefully the Motor Machine Gun Service list and there noted the announcement, "Keene, Louis, 2nd Lieut., to be 1st Lieut.," and for a fact this was the "official" intimation that I had been promoted. I had a couple of spare *pips*, rank stars, in my pocketbook, so I got my corporal to sew them on right away.

****

We are all very happy at times, very dirty, and covered with stings and bites; have no idea how long we are to remain up. Getting used to the shell fire, and can sleep through it if it's not too close. When it comes near it makes you very thoughtful. Still working at night and resting during the day. Made another emplacement for one of my machine guns last night; had twenty men digging; surprising how fast men dig when the bullets are flying.

****

It's about 2 a.m. We have just come in. My new emplacement is splendid; we've made it shell-proof and have it ready for firing. I was coming home this afternoon after having been to the fire trenches when I heard a shout: "Keene!"

I looked up on the canal bank and I saw the general with one of his A.D.C.'s sitting watching an aeroplane duel.

"I've come up to see your gun position, Keene."

I saluted, waited for him, and took him to it. It is below the level of the ground under tons of bricks in the ruins of a farmhouse. He was standing on the roof of it and said, "Well, where's the emplacement?"

"You're standing on it, sir."

"Tut, tut, 'pon my word, that's good." He was delighted and congratulated me on it.

My preliminary work under the eyes of the general has gone off quite well. I start firing tonight.

Intimacy between generals and lieutenants is unusual, but it looks as if mine had taken an interest in me, because when he noticed my insect-bitten face, he sent me down some dope he

200

had used with good effect in India. I expect the mosquitoes in India were the ordinary kind, but, believe me, trench "skeeters" are constructed differently and are proof against the general's pet concoction.

I have several miners in my section who take a personal pride in the digging and shoring up of dugouts. So far the other two sections of the Battery are always behind in this work but they may look better on parade.

The canal has one big lock suitable for swimming; a lot of "jocks" were bathing there today. I ordered a bathing parade for my section. Later I found that the swimming had livened three Germans, long submerged—the bathing parade is off.

A Belgian battery commander has just wakened up and his shells are rattling overhead. From the fire trenches an incessant rattle of rifles is heard; all the bullets seem to come over here; constantly the whine of a musical ricochet bullet is heard. Otherwise things are dead quiet. It's getting on for three, so I'm going to bed in my blankets on one of the late chateau owner's splendid spring mattresses and carved oak bedstead. Oh! how nice it would be to sleep without lice. From an adjoining cellar my section are snoring, and I'm going to add to the chorus. Good-night, everybody.

****

We have been having Sunday "hate." Eight-inch crumps are once more busting "up" the chateau. How they must detest this place. My tea and bully beef are covered with dust of the last shell. You have no idea how terrible the shell-fire is. First you hear the whistle and then a terrific burst which shakes the ground for a hundred yards around; when it clears away you find a hole ten feet across and six feet deep. At least fifteen have dropped around us in the last half hour.

This place isn't somewhere in France, it's somewhere in Hell! It has been the scene of a great many encounters; decayed French uniforms, old rifles, ammunition and leather equipment and bundles of mildewed tobacco leaves are strewn all over the place. I found the chin-strap of a German *Pickel-*

haube in the grounds, the helmet of a French cuirassier, and the red pants of a Zouave, close together. When digging in the trenches or anywhere near the firing line you have to be careful: corpses, dead horses, and cattle are buried everywhere. I'm building a trench to my emplacement and we have a stinking cow in the direct line; this will have to be buried before we can cut through.

Everybody is cheerful and going strong. Yesterday some of my men went swimming in the moat of the chateau; a shell dropped in the water near them, and threw up a lot of fish on to the bank. That kind of discouraged the Tommies swimming, so they cooked the fish and decided that safety comes before cleanliness out here.

It's hot and sticky, and when you have to wear thick clothes and equipment it makes you very uncomfortable, but it's all in the game.

All through the night we fired single shots from a machine gun; my orders were to fire between half-past eight at night and four o'clock in the morning. We have a number of guns doing this. It harasses the enemy and keeps them from sleeping; anything that will wear a man down is practiced here.

I've constructed a fire emplacement amongst the ruins underground; to get to it you have to travel through a tunnel eighteen feet long; inside it's very damp. I was working with my corporal, crouched up; we were both wet and cold, and so to cheer things up every now and again we let off a few rounds and warmed our hands on the barrel. Outside it poured with rain, and mosquitoes sought refuge inside and mealed off me. The corporal was immune. I had a water bottle full of whiskey and water. We used it to keep out the cold, but it wasn't strong enough. In a case like that you need wood alcohol. I would like to have had some Prohibitionists with me here. We had no light except the flash of the gun and the enemy star shells.

At daybreak I came home dead beat. I got into my cellar, was so tired that I threw myself down on the bed and wrapped myself up in my blankets, boots, mud, lice and all. I hadn't been asleep long before the Huns started "hating" the chateau. They have put over twenty-five large calibre shells into my place, the grounds and the house. They are still at it. Every time a shell bursts it makes a hole big enough to bury five horses, and it shakes the foundations all round. The shells are bigger than usual. The smoke and earth are blown up fifty or sixty feet in the air. The effect is a moral disruption. *Why can't they keep that cotton out of Germany?*

I have divided my section up into two teams, one in the cellars and one in the gun-pits. I relieve them every twenty-four hours, and I practically have to be in both places at once, but I have got a telephone in between the two places. I have it by my bed so that I can constantly know how things are going. However, the wire is cut two or three times a day by bullets and shell splinters, my linesman has a constant job.

Fired all night; came back at six o'clock this morning, very tired. Had a telegram from the general to fire two thousand rounds in twenty-four hours; this is quite hard work. Actually we could fire the lot in five minutes, but it would attract too much attention. The enemy use whole batteries of artillery to blot out machine guns which attract attention, so we have to fire single shots.

We have for neighbours four dead cows and an unexploded six-inch shell, liable to go off any time, all in a radius of one hundred yards. We have smashed holes through five walls so that we can go through the ruins unobserved. In one place we pass over a dead cow, and in another we wade through several tons of rotten potatoes, and I believe we have a corpse handy; and part of our trench goes through another heap of rotten mangles. I'm an authority on smells. I can almost tell the nationality of a corpse now by the smell. It will soon be necessary to wear our smoke-helmets to go into the emplacement. I don't think that I have told you that I cross the Yser canal about six times a day. I'd been up a week before I knew what it was. Now it only has a few feet of water in it, the rest being held in the German locks. The part I cross over is full of bulrushes, and is the home of moorhens, water rats, mosquitoes and frogs.

On one side of the canal is a bank which is in great demand by the machine gunners, who are able to get a certain amount of height and observation of their fire. The general has ordered a field gun to take up a position on this bank. He refers to it as his "Sniping eighteen-pounder." It is firing at seven hundred yards right at the German line and smashes up their parapet in a style that is pretty to watch. The machine gunners are in a great state, because the enemy will soon be "searching" with his artillery for the eighteen-pounder and the lairs of the smaller hidden guns will suffer.

The men are hunting for lice in their underwear. This is the kind of conversation that is coming through from the next cellars: "I've got you beat—that's forty-seven."

"Wait a minute"—a sound of tearing cloth—"but look at this lot, mother and young."

"With my forty and these you'll have to find some more."

They were betting on the number they could find. I peel off my shirt myself and burn them off with a candle. I glory in the little pop they make when the heat gets to them. All the insect powder in the world has been tried out on them and they've won.

All sentries here are doubled; one thing it's safer, and another it's company; even when things are quiet, rats and mice scamper about and it sets your nerves on end. Things which are inanimate during the day become alive at night. Trees seem to walk about. I wonder what it tastes like to have a real meal in which tinned food does not figure; fancy a tablecloth; my tablecloth is a double sheet of newspaper, and even then I can't have a new one every day.

****

Had a good night's rest; came in about twelve o'clock and slept until eight-thirty this morning. One eye is completely closed up by a sting.

A German aeroplane has been hovering over our positions looking for my gun, so we have stopped firing and all movement. I know just how the chicken feels when the hawk hovers over it. Few people realize how much aeroplanes figure in this war, for war would be much different without them. They do the work of Cavalry only in the sky. Whenever they come over, the sentries blow three blasts on their whistles and everybody runs for cover or freezes; guns stop firing and are covered up with branches made on frames. If men are caught in the open they stand perfectly still and do not look up, for on the aeroplane photographs faces at certain heights show light; dugouts are covered over with trees, straw or grass. We use aeroplane photographs a great deal; they show trenches distinctly and look very like the canals on Mars.

The Huns have been "hating" the road one quarter of a mile away all the morning. That doesn't worry us a bit as long as they don't come any closer. I'm willing always to share up on the shelling.

This order has just been issued. It speaks for itself:

All ranks are warned that bombs and grenades must not be used for fishing and killing game.

I went over another farm today. It is one of the well-ventilated kind, punched full of holes. In the kitchen, stables and outhouses there was a most wonderful collection of junk: ammunition, British and French bandoliers, old sheepskin coats abandoned by the British troops from last winter, smashed rifles, bayonets, meat tins, parts of broken equipment, sandbags, stacks of rotten potatoes and three dead cows. The fruit trees are laden with fruit, and vines are growing up the houses with their bunches of green grapes.

In the garden several lonely graves are piled high with old boots, straw, American agricultural implements, rotting sacks and rubbish of every description, pieces of shells, barrels, and in one room the rusty remains of a perambulator and sewing machine; rats are the only inhabitants now. In the garret (the staircase leading up to it gone long ago) I found a British rifle, bayonet fixed, ten rounds in the magazine, and the bolt partly drawn out. Evidently the owner was in the act of reloading his chamber when something happened. The graves were dated second and third months of this year. The poor wooden crosses were made of pieces of ration cases and the names written with an indelible pencil. The wretchedness of this farm, which was flourishing only a short time ago, is very pathetic.

We have adopted an old Belgian mother cat with her family of three kittens in the dugout. Now we find that three more little wild kittens are living in the bricks which we have piled around the windows to protect us against shells. They are all encouraged to live with us in the cellars. I like cats, and they will help to keep the rats down. Although some of the rats are nearly the size of cats.

It has been raining again and the trenches are filling up with slush. We carry a big trench stick, a thick sapling about four feet long with a ferrule made from a cartridge of a "very-light" (star shell), to help ourselves in walking; our feet are beginning to get wet and cold as a regular thing now, and we are revetting our trenches firm and solid for the winter. Eleven p.m. A mine under the Boche line has just been exploded. The fighting has just started for the crater.

I took a German Uhlan helmet from a gentleman who had no further use for it. It was pretty badly knocked about; still, if I can get it home it's a trophy.

****

It's about eight o'clock Sunday evening. All day long shells have been coming over like locomotives. Every five seconds one goes over into the old town; every five seconds for the last two hours. The chateau has been shelled again with "crumps"; they are such rotten shots; if only they would put in two good ones in the centre it would blow it to bits and then they might leave us alone. The whole of the ground is pitted because they can't hit it squarely.

****

My work lies behind the front line and in front of the support, firing over the heads of the men in the main trenches. The emplacement was shelled today; one shell hit the roof, burst and knocked over one of my men, cutting his head open. He is not very badly hurt, but has gone to the hospital. The shelling has been terrible today.

MR. TOMMY ATKINS

The Germans have been very quiet lately, and working parties are out all along their front lines at night—something's up. Dirty work can be expected at any time now. We have steel helmets to protect us from spent bullets and splinters. They look like the old Tudor steel helmets and they are fine to wash in.

You have no idea what a big part food plays in our life. Yesterday morning I went with the machine-gun officer of another outfit to crawl about looking for positions. We were in an orchard. I happened to look up and saw ripe plums! Terrified lest he should see them and forestall me, I said, "Let's beat it, this is too unhealthy," so we crawled back. Last night in the light of a big moon such as coons always steal watermelons by, a section officer and his cook crawled to the plum tree. The section officer, being large, stood underneath while the cook climbed the tree and dropped them into a sandbag held open by the S.O. They got about ten pounds. They go well stewed, believe me. The fact that bullets whistled through the trees most of the time made them taste better today. Sat the rest of the night in a hedge firing at the Boches with a Lewis gun. I struck for bed just as dawn broke.

****

Today the guns are again "hating" the chateau, and they have put sixty shells in the neighbourhood. Still, "there's no cloud without a silver lining." I've got a new way home. Instead of going right around the kennels, stables, and through the yards, I go "through" the greenhouse direct, thereby saving a lot of time. The Huns' calendar is wrong. They have always shelled me Sunday and Wednesday. Today's Tuesday!

We use up the window frames and doorways for kindling, and consequently the doors have gone long ago. I have been smashing up mouldings this morning with an axe. We prefer the dry wood which is built into the walls; it burns better and doesn't cause smoke. As soon as smoke is seen rising, the enemy's range-finders get busy and then we suffer.

Another mine went up yesterday; nobody seems to know where. I think it came south from the French lines; it rocked the whole neighbourhood for miles. The ground here is a kind of quicksand for a few feet down, and shock is easily transmitted, the whole ground being honeycombed with mines, old trenches, shafts, saps made by French, Belgians, Germans and our own people.

The use for timber of any description is manifold; every little bit is used up. Our chief source of supply of dry wood is from the smashed-up chateaux. Langhof, my home, has been punished almost every day, and after the bombardment lets up men from the neighbourhood come to collect the wood torn up by the shelling. The men of the Tenth East Yorks came up this morning and climbed to the remains of the second story, ripping up the floor boards. The enemy evidently saw them, for the shelling soon started. We have been shelled often here before, but it was nothing compared to this. The shells were carefully placed and came over with disgusting regularity. The buildings rocked and the whole neighbourhood shook. Fountains of bricks, mortar, and dirt were spewed up into the air. Trees were torn to shreds, a wall in front of me was hit—and disappeared, a lead statue of Apollo in the garden was hurled through the air and landed fifty yards away crumpled up against the balustrade of the moat.

We were in our cellars, and gradually the shelling crept up towards us. Slowly a solemn dread which soon moulded into a sordid fear took possession of my being. In a flash I began to devise a philosophy of death for my chances were fading with every crash. I took out my pocketbook, containing some letters from my mother and some personal things, and put them on one of the beams, so that, being in another part of the building, they might perhaps be found some day. The shelling continued and shells dropped completely round the cellars, demolishing nearly everything in sight. The enemy evidently wanted to obliterate the whole place. The smell of the smoke and the dirt from the debris was choking, and every minute we expected to be our last. Suddenly it stopped. Philosophy and fear disappeared simultaneously as I sputtered out a choking laugh of relief. Then Hawkins, my servant, in a scared voice started, and the others joined in, singing the old marching refrain of the Training Camps:

Hail, hail, the gang's all here,
What the hell do we care!
What the hell do we care!
Hail, hail, the gang's all here,
What the hell do we care now!

When a man has lived night after night in a trench, he gradually finds it quite possible to snatch a good night's sleep. In other words, it is merely a case of becoming acclimated to rackets, smells and food. I had always been able to sleep, but on the night following the bombardment of the chateau I just could not doze off. I thrashed about continuously, and while in this restless state harboured the notion that trouble was brewing for me. Every one has had that feeling, the feeling that hangs in your bones and warns you to watch out. Well, that is how I felt.

At last the sun rose and with it came a beautiful morning, warm and sunny. I walked out amongst the ruins to see the extent of the damage caused by the shelling of the previous day. I was waiting for the stew which was cooking on a little fire near the side of the cellar. The "dixie" was resting on two old bayonets, and they in turn rested on bricks at either side. Towards noon a big shell came over and landed in the moat, covering everything around with a coat of evil-smelling, black mud. This shell was followed by another, arriving in the part of the ruins where once a cow-shed stood. I was talking to Hawkins, my batman, when I saw him dive across my front and fall flat on his face. At the same time I was in the centre of an explosion, a great flame of light and then bricks, wood and cement flew in all directions. For a few seconds I thought I was dead, then I picked myself up and saw that blood was pouring down the front of my jacket. I followed up the stream and found that my right hand was smashed and hanging limp. My men rushed out and I told them it was nothing, but promptly fell in a heap. When I came to, my hand was wrapped up in an emergency bandage, and a stretcher was coming down from

Bedford House, an advanced dressing-station, the next house back. To the delight of the men who were carrying it, I waved them away and told them I could walk. Assisted up to the dressing-station by one of my men, I made it. I then made a discovery. A soldier is a man until he's hit, then he's a case. I first had an injection of "anti-tetanus" in the side, and the fact was recorded on a label tied to my left-hand top pocket button. The doctor tied me up, then said: "You'll soon be all right. Will you have a bottle of English beer or a drop of whiskey?" I had the whiskey. I needed it. All the time I was there the wounded poured in. Seeing them I felt ashamed to be there with only a smashed hand. A corporal came in with both hands blown off and fifty-six other wounds. He had tried to save the men in his bay by throwing back a German bomb and it had gone off in his hands. Hawkins came up later on with my helmet and the fuse head of the shell which blew me up. We were all collected together and waited in the dugouts of the dressing station until dusk. Several shells came close to us. I tried to write to my mother with my left hand, so that when she received the War Office cable she would know I was able to write.

Dusk came, then night, and finally the Ford ambulance cars which were to take us out of Hell. It was a beautiful night. Belgium looked lovely. The merciful night had thrown a veil over the war scars on the land and a moon was shining. I was told to sit up in the seat with the driver. We travelled along one road, then the shelling became so bad that the drivers decided to go back and take another road which was running nearly parallel. Back over the line the planes of the Royal Flying Corps were bombing the Forest of Houltholst, and the bursting of the shrapnel from the German anti-aircraft guns pierced the velvet of the sky like stars as we went out of Belgium into France.

****

Several times shells burst on the road, and from the inside of the car came the stifled groans of the men as the Ford hit limbs of trees and shell-holes.

Our first stop was a ruined windmill, the walls of which

were nearly six feet thick. Here the dangerous cases were taken off and attended to. The last I saw of the corporal was after they had cut off his coat at the seams and the doctors were taking a piece of wire out of his chest. While I was waiting a chaplain asked me if I would like a cup of coffee or some whiskey, realising that it would take some time to get the coffee made I had some more whiskey.

I was given two more tags, which this time were tied on buttons at the top of my jacket. I stayed here about two hours, then I was sent to a clearing hospital. It was here that I met the first nurses. They were two fine, splendid women who were wearing the scarlet hoods of the British Regular Army nurse. They were both strong and quite capable of handling a man, even if he became delirious. One of them quickly got me into bed. I apologized for my terribly dirty state, but I was told that it made no difference; they were used to it. To be between clean sheets again was wonderful. I felt I wanted to go to sleep forever. Suddenly a roar, and a terrible explosion. The hospital was being bombed; a bomb had dropped within a hundred yards of my tent. This was the German reprisal for our bombing Houltholst. They deliberately bombed a hospital. The doctor at this hospital next day looked at my hand and said in a nonchalant way, "Looks as though you will lose it." At that time it didn't strike me as a great loss to lose a hand, even if it was my "painting hand."

The hospital train of the next day was crowded and the nurse in charge of my coach was named Keene. We tried in the little spare time she had to see if we couldn't work out our genealogy and find out if we were even remotely connected, but before we did we came to the station of Etaples and then went to the Duchess of Westminster Hospital at Latouquet. Here I was operated on. A piece of Krupp's steel was taken out of my hand and a rubber drainage tube inserted instead. The Duchess used to come round a great deal and won everybody's affection. She used to sit on my bed and talk to me about pleasant things. So unlike many people who visit hospitals and ask the patients silly war questions, such as:

"How does it feel to be wounded?"

"Which hurts more, a bayonet or a shell wound?"

One exasperated Tommy, when asked if the shell hit him, said:

"Naw, it crept up behind and bit me."

LEONAUR

ALSO FROM LEONAUR
AVAILABLE IN SOFTCOVER OR HARDCOVER WITH DUST JACKET

THE FALL OF THE MOGHUL EMPIRE OF HINDUSTAN *by H. G. Keene*—
By the beginning of the nineteenth century, as British and Indian armies under Lake and Wellesley dominated the scene, a little over half a century of conflict brought the Moghul Empire to its knees.

LADY SALE'S AFGHANISTAN *by Florentia Sale*—An Indomitable Victorian Lady's Account of the Retreat from Kabul During the First Afghan War.

THE CAMPAIGN OF MAGENTA AND SOLFERINO 1859 *by Harold Carmichael Wylly*—The Decisive Conflict for the Unification of Italy.

FRENCH'S CAVALRY CAMPAIGN *by J. G. Maydon*—A Special Correspondent's View of British Army Mounted Troops During the Boer War.

CAVALRY AT WATERLOO *by Sir Evelyn Wood*—British Mounted Troops During the Campaign of 1815.

THE SUBALTERN *by George Robert Gleig*—The Experiences of an Officer of the 85th Light Infantry During the Peninsular War.

NAPOLEON AT BAY, 1814 *by F. Loraine Petre*—The Campaigns to the Fall of the First Empire.

NAPOLEON AND THE CAMPAIGN OF 1806 *by Colonel Vachée*—The Napoleonic Method of Organisation and Command to the Battles of Jena & Auerstädt.

THE COMPLETE ADVENTURES IN THE CONNAUGHT RANGERS *by William Grattan*—The 88th Regiment during the Napoleonic Wars by a Serving Officer.

BUGLER AND OFFICER OF THE RIFLES *by William Green & Harry Smith*—With the 95th (Rifles) during the Peninsular & Waterloo Campaigns of the Napoleonic Wars.

NAPOLEONIC WAR STORIES *by Sir Arthur Quiller-Couch*—Tales of soldiers, spies, battles & sieges from the Peninsular & Waterloo campaigns.

CAPTAIN OF THE 95TH (RIFLES) *by Jonathan Leach*—An officer of Wellington's sharpshooters during the Peninsular, South of France and Waterloo campaigns of the Napoleonic wars.

RIFLEMAN COSTELLO *by Edward Costello*—The adventures of a soldier of the 95th (Rifles) in the Peninsular & Waterloo Campaigns of the Napoleonic wars.

ALSO FROM LEONAUR
AVAILABLE IN SOFTCOVER OR HARDCOVER WITH DUST JACKET

ZULU:1879 *by D.C.F. Moodie & the Leonaur Editors*—The Anglo-Zulu War of 1879 from contemporary sources: First Hand Accounts, Interviews, Dispatches, Official Documents & Newspaper Reports.

THE RED DRAGOON *by W.J. Adams*—With the 7th Dragoon Guards in the Cape of Good Hope against the Boers & the Kaffir tribes during the 'war of the axe' 1843-48'.

THE RECOLLECTIONS OF SKINNER OF SKINNER'S HORSE *by James Skinner*—James Skinner and his 'Yellow Boys' Irregular cavalry in the wars of India between the British, Mahratta, Rajput, Mogul, Sikh & Pindarree Forces.

A CAVALRY OFFICER DURING THE SEPOY REVOLT *by A. R. D. Mackenzie*—Experiences with the 3rd Bengal Light Cavalry, the Guides and Sikh Irregular Cavalry from the outbreak to Delhi and Lucknow.

A NORFOLK SOLDIER IN THE FIRST SIKH WAR *by J W Baldwin*—Experiences of a private of H.M. 9th Regiment of Foot in the battles for the Punjab, India 1845-6.

TOMMY ATKINS' WAR STORIES: 14 FIRST HAND ACCOUNTS—Fourteen first hand accounts from the ranks of the British Army during Queen Victoria's Empire.

THE WATERLOO LETTERS *by H. T. Siborne*—Accounts of the Battle by British Officers for its Foremost Historian.

NEY: GENERAL OF CAVALRY VOLUME 1—1769-1799 *by Antoine Bulos*—The Early Career of a Marshal of the First Empire.

NEY: MARSHAL OF FRANCE VOLUME 2—1799-1805 *by Antoine Bulos*—The Early Career of a Marshal of the First Empire.

AIDE-DE-CAMP TO NAPOLEON *by Philippe-Paul de Ségur*—For anyone interested in the Napoleonic Wars this book, written by one who was intimate with the strategies and machinations of the Emperor, will be essential reading.

TWILIGHT OF EMPIRE *by Sir Thomas Ussher & Sir George Cockburn*—Two accounts of Napoleon's Journeys in Exile to Elba and St. Helena: Narrative of Events by Sir Thomas Ussher & Napoleon's Last Voyage: Extract of a diary by Sir George Cockburn.

PRIVATE WHEELER *by William Wheeler*—The letters of a soldier of the 51st Light Infantry during the Peninsular War & at Waterloo.

LEONAUR

ALSO FROM LEONAUR
AVAILABLE IN SOFTCOVER OR HARDCOVER WITH DUST JACKET

THE RELUCTANT REBEL *by William G. Stevenson*—A young Kentuckian's experiences in the Confederate Infantry & Cavalry during the American Civil War..

BOOTS AND SADDLES *by Elizabeth B. Custer*—The experiences of General Custer's Wife on the Western Plains.

FANNIE BEERS' CIVIL WAR *by Fannie A. Beers*—A Confederate Lady's Experiences of Nursing During the Campaigns & Battles of the American Civil War.

LADY SALE'S AFGHANISTAN *by Florentia Sale*—An Indomitable Victorian Lady's Account of the Retreat from Kabul During the First Afghan War.

THE TWO WARS OF MRS DUBERLY *by Frances Isabella Duberly*—An Intrepid Victorian Lady's Experience of the Crimea and Indian Mutiny.

THE REBELLIOUS DUCHESS *by Paul F. S. Dermoncourt*—The Adventures of the Duchess of Berri and Her Attempt to Overthrow French Monarchy.

LADIES OF WATERLOO *by Charlotte A. Eaton, Magdalene de Lancey & Juana Smith*—The Experiences of Three Women During the Campaign of 1815: Waterloo Days by Charlotte A. Eaton, A Week at Waterloo by Magdalene de Lancey & Juana's Story by Juana Smith.

TWO YEARS BEFORE THE MAST *by Richard Henry Dana. Jr.*—The account of one young man's experiences serving on board a sailing brig—the Penelope—bound for California, between the years1834-36.

A SAILOR OF KING GEORGE *by Frederick Hoffman*—From Midshipman to Captain—Recollections of War at Sea in the Napoleonic Age 1793-1815.

LORDS OF THE SEA *by A. T. Mahan*—Great Captains of the Royal Navy During the Age of Sail.

COGGESHALL'S VOYAGES: VOLUME 1 *by George Coggeshall*—The Recollections of an American Schooner Captain.

COGGESHALL'S VOYAGES: VOLUME 2 *by George Coggeshall*—The Recollections of an American Schooner Captain.

TWILIGHT OF EMPIRE *by Sir Thomas Ussher & Sir George Cockburn*—Two accounts of Napoleon's Journeys in Exile to Elba and St. Helena: Narrative of Events by Sir Thomas Ussher & Napoleon's Last Voyage: Extract of a diary by Sir George Cockburn.

LEONAUR

ALSO FROM LEONAUR
AVAILABLE IN SOFTCOVER OR HARDCOVER WITH DUST JACKET

ESCAPE FROM THE FRENCH *by Edward Boys*—A Young Royal Navy Midshipman's Adventures During the Napoleonic War.

THE VOYAGE OF H.M.S. PANDORA *by Edward Edwards R. N. & George Hamilton, edited by Basil Thomson*—In Pursuit of the Mutineers of the Bounty in the South Seas—1790-1791.

MEDUSA *by J. B. Henry Savigny and Alexander Correard and Charlotte-Adélaïde Dard* —Narrative of a Voyage to Senegal in 1816 & The Sufferings of the Picard Family After the Shipwreck of the Medusa.

THE SEA WAR OF 1812 VOLUME 1 *by A. T. Mahan*—A History of the Maritime Conflict.

THE SEA WAR OF 1812 VOLUME 2 *by A. T. Mahan*—A History of the Maritime Conflict.

WETHERELL OF H. M. S. HUSSAR *by John Wetherell*—The Recollections of an Ordinary Seaman of the Royal Navy During the Napoleonic Wars.

THE NAVAL BRIGADE IN NATAL *by C. R. N. Burne*—With the Guns of H. M. S. Terrible & H. M. S. Tartar during the Boer War 1899-1900.

THE VOYAGE OF H. M. S. BOUNTY *by William Bligh*—The True Story of an 18th Century Voyage of Exploration and Mutiny.

SHIPWRECK! *by William Gilly*—The Royal Navy's Disasters at Sea 1793-1849.

KING'S CUTTERS AND SMUGGLERS: 1700-1855 *by E. Keble Chatterton*—A unique period of maritime history-from the beginning of the eighteenth to the middle of the nineteenth century when British seamen risked all to smuggle valuable goods from wool to tea and spirits from and to the Continent.

CONFEDERATE BLOCKADE RUNNER *by John Wilkinson*—The Personal Recollections of an Officer of the Confederate Navy.

NAVAL BATTLES OF THE NAPOLEONIC WARS *by W. H. Fitchett*—Cape St. Vincent, the Nile, Cadiz, Copenhagen, Trafalgar & Others.

PRISONERS OF THE RED DESERT *by R. S. Gwatkin-Williams*—The Adventures of the Crew of the Tara During the First World War.

U-BOAT WAR 1914-1918 *by James B. Connolly/Karl von Schenk*—Two Contrasting Accounts from Both Sides of the Conflict at Sea D uring the Great War.

LEONAUR

ALSO FROM LEONAUR
AVAILABLE IN SOFTCOVER OR HARDCOVER WITH DUST JACKET

FARAWAY CAMPAIGN *by F. James*—Experiences of an Indian Army Cavalry Officer in Persia & Russia During the Great War.

REVOLT IN THE DESERT *by T. E. Lawrence*—An account of the experiences of one remarkable British officer's war from his own perspective.

MACHINE-GUN SQUADRON *by A. M. G.*—The 20th Machine Gunners from British Yeomanry Regiments in the Middle East Campaign of the First World War.

A GUNNER'S CRUSADE *by Antony Bluett*—The Campaign in the Desert, Palestine & Syria as Experienced by the Honourable Artillery Company During the Great War .

DESPATCH RIDER *by W. H. L. Watson*—The Experiences of a British Army Motorcycle Despatch Rider During the Opening Battles of the Great War in Europe.

TIGERS ALONG THE TIGRIS *by E. J. Thompson*—The Leicestershire Regiment in Mesopotamia During the First World War.

HEARTS & DRAGONS *by Charles R. M. F. Crutwell*—The 4th Royal Berkshire Regiment in France and Italy During the Great War, 1914-1918.

INFANTRY BRIGADE: 1914 *by John Ward*—The Diary of a Commander of the 15th Infantry Brigade, 5th Division, British Army, During the Retreat from Mons.

DOING OUR 'BIT' *by Ian Hay*—Two Classic Accounts of the Men of Kitchener's 'New Army' During the Great War including *The First 100,000* & *All In It*.

AN EYE IN THE STORM *by Arthur Ruhl*—An American War Correspondent's Experiences of the First World War from the Western Front to Gallipoli-and Beyond.

STAND & FALL *by Joe Cassells*—With the Middlesex Regiment Against the Bolsheviks 1918-19.

RIFLEMAN MACGILL'S WAR *by Patrick MacGill*—A Soldier of the London Irish During the Great War in Europe including *The Amateur Army*, *The Red Horizon* & *The Great Push*.

WITH THE GUNS *by C. A. Rose & Hugh Dalton*—Two First Hand Accounts of British Gunners at War in Europe During World War 1- Three Years in France with the Guns and With the British Guns in Italy.

THE BUSH WAR DOCTOR *by Robert V. Dolbey*—The Experiences of a British Army Doctor During the East African Campaign of the First World War.